AF732415

Fairest Girlhood

In the *Clarion Classics* series:

- *The Abiding Presence*, Hugh Martin
- *The Complete Green Letters*, Miles J. Stanford
- *Confession and Forgiveness*, Andrew Murray
- *The Confessions of St. Augustine in Modern English*, Sherwood E. Wirt, translator
- *Fairest Girlhood*, Margaret E. Sangster
- *Fox's Book of Martyrs*, W. B. Forbush, editor
- *George Muller of Bristol*, Arthur T. Pierson
- *God's Best Secrets*, Andrew Murray
- *Great Thoughts from the Upper Room*, F. B. Meyer
- *How to Live a Victorious Life*, an unknown Christian
- *The Imitation of Christ*, Thomas á Kempis
- *In His Steps*, Charles M. Sheldon
- *The Inner Life*, Andrew Murray
- *The Kneeling Christian*, an unknown Christian
- *Mary Slessor of Calabar*, W. P. Livingstone
- *The Power-Filled Christian*, an unknown Christian
- *The Prayers of Susanna Wesley*, W. L. Doughty, editor
- *Robert Murray McCheyne*, A. A. Bonar
- *The Spirit of Prayer*, Hannah More
- *Spiritual Letters to Women*, Francois Fenelon
- *They Found the Secret*, Raymond V. Edman
- *With Christ in the School of Prayer*, Andrew Murray

Fairest Girlhood

Margaret E. Sangster

CLARION CLASSICS
Zondervan Publishing House
Grand Rapids, Michigan

First published in 1906 by Fleming H. Revell

Clarion Classics are published by
Zondervan Publishing House,
1415 Lake Drive, S.E.,
Grand Rapids, Michigan 49506

Library of Congress Cataloging in Publication Data

Sangster, Margaret Elizabeth Munson, 1838-1912
Fairest girlhood.

Reprint. Originally published: Old Tappan, N.J.: F.H. Revell, 1906.

1. Young women–Religious life. 2. Young women–conduct of life. I. Title.

BV4551.S26 1986 248.8'33 86-14615
ISBN 0-310-34471-9

Designed by Ann Cherryman

Printed in the United States of America

86 87 88 89 90 91 / ZO / 10 9 8 7 6 5 4 3 2 1

To my friend
Grace H. Dodge

Contents

Foreword

That our daughters may be as cornerstones polished after the similitude of a palace! Many centuries ago the sweet singer of Israel uttered this wish, and ever since it has been inwoven with the most sacred ideal of the human heart. Our daughters are the most precious of our treasures, the dearest possessions of our homes, and the objects of our most watchful love. Beyond this, they are to the family and the race as cornerstones on which depend the integrity and beauty of the social edifice.

If an apology were needed for modestly adding another to the number of books written especially for girls, I might make it in a single sentence. So much of my life has been devoted to work among girls, so large is the circle of whom I think as I write to them, and so intimate is my knowledge of their hopes and aims that I am assured of a hearing when I send forth this little book.

Girls have written to me from every state in the Union, and from every country on the globe. They have admitted me to their fellowship in colleges, schools, conferences, and places of toil. I have broken bread with them at the noon hour in the factory. I have sat by their side in the restroom at the Christian Association. I have talked with them at Northfield, Asheville, and Silver Bay in the summer gloaming. I have looked upon their faces in chapel and have chatted with them under the trees and in girls' rooms where, when the seats were filled, they gathered about me on the floor. I think I know our girls of today. I have not forgotten how I felt when I was myself a girl. Their trials and triumphs, their hopes and aspirations, their ambitions and fulfillments are interesting and important in my eyes. As they are in the fairest and most winsome season of life, and as no human foresight can tell what the future may hold for them, I can but trust that every girl who reads this book may have a life filled to the brim with usefulness and may have all the joy in living that our Father can give her.

The book is not alone for the college girl, the working girl, the home girl, or the business girl. It has been written with love in every line for all sorts and conditions of girls, for the Fairest Girlhood in the world.

—Margaret E. Sangster

Chapter I

The New Penelope

PENELOPE, by right of her eighteen beautiful years, has a wider viewpoint than any maid who ever lived before her. She may not realize it, indeed, how should she, but her world is not the same that her mother faced in her teens, nor is it the world of her grandmother's girlhood, nor of a single Penelope of the past. There is a portrait by Copley on the drawing room wall, the pride and boast of the family, and it represents the colonial ancestress who entertained General Washington after the long war with England, a great lady whose daughters danced the minuet with his gallant young officers. That Penelope was painted in her girlhood when she had brown eyes and a dimple in her chin; her hair was dressed high and powdered, and she had ringlets shading her rounded cheeks; her dress was short-waisted and of shimmering satin; her look was haughty, but something in it tempered with sweetness has descended to this girl of ours, who plays golf and tennis with an energy that would have startled the belle of seventy-six. The belle of the eighteenth century was a trifle weak in her spelling. Her descendant could not blunder if she tried.

Through the passing years the house has always had a daughter named Penelope as other houses have their fair succession of Eleanors, Dorothys, Margarets, and Marions. One Penelope repeats the characteristics of another or accentuates them by contrast. When the summer daisies return with June, in all the waving fields, they are precisely alike, petal for petal, disc for disc, and as the daisies were fifty years ago, the daisies are today. But girls show similarity in many ways yet preserve each and all a beautiful individuality, with only now and then so complete a reversion to type that it is to the onlooker as if the latest daughter of the house were a reincarnation of her great-grandmother. Quaint, willful, capricious, resourceful, many-sided, our Penelope of the hour equals or surpasses those who preceded her by so much as her advantages are greater and her opportunities multiplied a thousandfold.

Every generation climbs to its own hilltop and from thence surveys the landscape o'er. And it does not see what the people saw who have been there and have gone away and left the field clear for the dreamers, the fighters, and the toilers of the present. Yesterday is not today, as today will not be tomorrow, though every yesterday since the world was made has some stake in today and some investment in tomorrow.

What does our Penelope see from her hill?

She sees certain things that are tangible and certain others that are spiritual.

First of all before Penelope's young eyes there spreads a world of enchanting possibilities and broadening hope, a world of which the key is in the hand of the young girl. Never hitherto was girlhood left so free to find its fit expression; never could it do so readily all that it desired, and never had it a choice among so many careers. The modern world may be material, it may be bent on the accumulation of wealth, it may march to its own ends with a celerity and a cruelty that trample down the feeble not only without remorse but without regret, yet in one particular it is a world of chivalry. It exalts The Young Girl, regards her foibles indulgently, and delights in letting her carry out her plans and fulfill her missions. The twentieth-century world is at the feet of The Young Girl.

Penelope may prefer to live in the sheltered seclusion of her home, ministering there to her dear ones and being the angel of the fireside. She may feel that her life will be incomplete and dwarfed unless she can use the powers God has given her in a profession or business that has to do with the world's work. She may long to show of what stuff she is made. As she looks from her hilltop, across the world which awaits her, beyond the mystic boundary line between girlhood and womanhood she beholds a realm which has on every side legitimate outlets for activity and invitations to expansion.

Other Penelopes gazed upon the world through little panes of glass, set high in a tower window. They waved their hands to cheer the knights who went forth to battle, following them with wistful glances as they disappeared around a turn of the road in quest of brave adventures. This Penelope climbs no turret stair. She is herself in the open, under heaven's own blue, and may go forward on her path as dauntlessly as every hero did in the Middle Ages. Heroines today are better off than heroes and have as few limitations. One does not often hear a girl lament that she is not a boy, a lament once common.

Penelope's world may be the world of the scholar, of the trained nurse, of the physician, the artist, the poet, the traveler, or the homemaker. It shall be the world of her heart's desire. It is a goodly land on which the modern girl gazes, a world which is very wide-awake and has not many illusions, although it is on the whole a bright and happy world with tremendous problems that do not overwhelm it and a movement timed by steam and electricity.

As for the intangible, Penelope is aware of changes which

though invisible are none the less actual. For one thing she need be in no hurry. The old system drew hard and fast lines around girlhood. From sixteen to twenty was the period of girlish bloom and hope. I met the other day a middle-aged woman who told me that she was a bride at fifteen. The beautiful mother of a bevy of beautiful girls, friends of my early youth, was wedded on her sixteenth birthday. Another woman, not yet old, put up her hair for the first time on the day when as a little bride of seventeen, she was married to a man of forty whom she had known for only three months. She said, "I cried when my mother said that I could not any longer wear my hair in braids hanging down my back. My wedding gown was my first trained dress." This girl was probably extremely childish at seventeen and had little voice in her marriage. The dread of Penelope used to be that she would slip out of her teens and into her twenties before she could assume the state of the matron. An unmarried girl at twenty-five was unique, an object of pity, of wondering comment. Her parents were secretly commiserated. She was made painfully conscious of the pressure of the surrounding atmosphere, that she belonged to the army of those who were unsought.

Fortunately we have changed all that. Our girls need not hasten out of their fairyland. They go to school and stay there a long time after they have reached their teens. Eighteen is the average entrance age for college, and twenty-two the average age of graduation. A young woman is as fearlessly youthful at twenty-seven as she formerly was at eighteen. In consequence Penelope from her hilltop looks confidently forward to a long and cheery girlhood.

She sees, too, that her opinions and convictions must count for a great deal in their effect upon her friends. If she is steadfast and pure hearted with a high ideal of honor and an unfaltering faith in God, she will inevitably elevate the standards of those around her. The men she meets, those of her own family and immediate circle or those who may be her business associates, derive their conception of womanhood from her. If, therefore, she shall begin her life by dedicating it to the service of Jesus Christ, walking through the world with Him as her guide, she will give tone to all who come within the sphere of her influence. In Penelope's case the things that are seen are temporal but the things that are not seen are eternal.

We are in the habit of saying and thinking that the other sex counts for very little with the modern Penelope. Yet is this quite true? Is not nature more potential than modern theories? Our girls are ambitious to make their own way, to earn their own money, to possess their independence, and they are accused a little unfairly of restlessness because they are sometimes reluctant to stay at home in luxury and idleness when every pulse of their being thrills with an intense longing for action. There are all sorts and conditions of girls in Penelope's world. Some are morbid, some are unreasonable, some are heedless, some are vain and silly. Here and there one is, it may be, a little stupid, measured by the exacting canons of the brilliant sisterhood about her. Some have one talent, others have ten. You cannot with justice blame a young girl if she does not particularly enjoy washing dishes and darning stockings. If, on occasion, she performs these tasks without needless fretting, she has done her duty. If these homely occupations are not her real work, why should she be compelled to spend her life over them when she may do other and more congenial things that will tell to better results. Every girl is not fitted with the talents that make for domesticity; yet singularly when the time comes the woman-side of a girl's nature unfolds under the subtle potency of love as the flower unfolds in the sun. Penelope may have been a blue-stocking or a genius. It is quite possible that she shall in due time preside at her table; order her household, and bless the life of her husband as fully as though she had never written a story or painted a picture or molded a statue.

In Penelope's balancing scales, home does not always weigh as heavily as it should while she is immature. A young girl comes by degrees into her kingdom. With her, day is at the dawn. All about her are tints of rose and pearl and songs of birds and sparkle of dew and scent of a thousand flowers. She is not wholly awake in the dawn. Dreams have woven a spell around her and the dreams are not always of things beyond herself. Of necessity a young girl's life is self-centered. Little by little she emerges into a region where she values life most as it touches other lives.

Penelope need not be hurried. We do not want hothouse forcing for our girl. We are willing to wait until Nature shapes her as she was meant to be.

"Queen-rose of the rosebud garden of girls," the daughter of the house is its most precious possession. At one time there was a feeling on the part of fathers and brothers that come what might she must be sheltered from the winds of adversity.

Within a twelvemonth a southern gentleman of the old school said in my hearing, "While I live and my boys live no daughter of mine shall go out of the house to work for her bread."

Misfortune had overtaken the family and financial ruin was impending. A friend innocently asked why do not the girls learn something by which they may support themselves. They had received a somewhat superficial education and were not yet fitted in any way to cope with the world although they were lovely in manner and well taught in social accomplishments. I shall not soon forget their father's resentment at the bare mention of their leaving the home roof for any reason except that of marriage. I know more than one courtly man with silver hair of whom in his youth it was freely said that he had remained a bachelor that he might take care of an impoverished mother and sisters.

The Penelope of today will not consent to be a makeweight on her brother, nor will she deign to handicap him so long as she has health and strength and a disciplined mind. There are exceptions, but they are few.

Teachers tell me that the girls of the hour are a trifle less spontaneous and less enthusiastic than girls were ten or fifteen years ago, and they lay the blame for this at the door of the home. They say with conviction that home life is less thoughtful, less spiritual than in days when every home had its family altar and everywhere fathers and mothers deemed it of the first consequence that their daughters should blossom into Christian womanhood. There are mothers whose solicitude for Penelope is that she shall shine in the drawing room, and they are willing to sacrifice real culture on her part to this end. One teacher observed sorrowfully, "The mothers are more to blame than the daughters if the daughters are shallow."

Another commenting in the same vein added, "Girls are blasé; they have too many pleasures thrust upon them from the nursery onward, and it is difficult to awaken them to delight in work. But," she added, "it can be done and when it is done there is no finer specimen in the world than the girl of today."

I have heard these expressions, but with an interrogation point. To my mind girls are always lovable, susceptible of receiving and retaining the happiest impressions, and are responsive to the best that can be offered them. May it not be once in a while that teachers are tired or that they drift into the error of investing the past with an atmosphere of romance? Penelope as she stands before me in the first decade of the twentieth century a "sweet girl graduate in her golden hair," an earnest businesswoman, a gifted artist or poet, a consecrated Christian worker, or just a daughter at home, is the dearest and most beautiful being on the planet, a girl with life beckoning her and heaven arching above her head.

Chapter II

The Old-Fashioned Schoolgirl

THE YOUNG LADIES' SEMINARY or more old-fashioned still, The Female Academy of our grandparents' day survives only in the recollections of very aged people and in books written in the early nineteenth century. When this republic was in its infancy girls by courtesy were permitted to share the studies of their brothers, but the ideal education for the daughter was domestic. The term "blue stocking" was one of reproach and Miss Edgeworth, although the daughter of a man whose ideas were in advance of his period, in more than one story expressed the opinion of the time in reference to girls who studied Latin when they ought to have been doing fine needlework.

Gradually a change came over the minds of thinking people, and it was not considered reprehensible to give a clever and ambitious girl a chance to learn whatever she desired provided her chance did not take one from a clever and ambitious boy in the same household. It is within the memory of persons little past their prime that strenuous opposition was made to the modern woman's college, many people fearing that it would ruin girls for home life, permanently unsettle them, or make them mannish. This notion has been dissipated as it has been shown conclusively that girls may have disciplined brains and remain womanly and that the alumnae of Vassar, Smith, Wellesley, Mount Holyoke, and other colleges are among the most attractive and charming young women the country produces.

An equally fine type of girlhood is graduated from schools of a high rank, giving elective courses while not insisting on the full curriculum of the college.

If, however, our modern Penelope has a fancy that her grandmother and her great-aunt and the women of a day still earlier than theirs were superficially prepared for life, were shallow and brainless and very wretchedly taught, let her be undeceived. The modern girl has no monopoly on what may be called a liberal education. The education of the former day differed in detail from ours yet in essentials it was thorough and its effects on character were enduring and elevating.

A pioneer in American education was the Rev. Joseph Emerson. He saw with clear vision the necessity of educating woman in order that she might fill nobly her office as educator. His motto was, "To do the greatest good to the greatest number, for the longest time." From his academy he sent forth many admirable teachers, among whom were Zilpah P. Grant and Mary Lyon.

Miss Lyon has the enduring honor of having founded Mount Holyoke. Miss Grant, who was perhaps one of the most remarkable teachers of her own or any period, became the successor of Mr. Emerson at Ipswich. By the kindness of my friend Miss Susan Hayes Ward I am permitted to quote from letters preserved in her family. These letters were written respectively to a brother and a mother, the writers being students in Miss Grant's school and both on the borderland of sixteen.

I may add that great emphasis was placed by Miss Grant on religious education and on Bible study. Every day began with a definite study of a portion of the Bible, and in every way possible the spirituality of her pupils was deepened and they were encouraged to feel the responsibility of life. She aimed to educate teachers. Her constant endeavor was to make each girl do her best and her severest censure was given to one who had not done the best of which she was capable.

In those simple days bills for tuition were very low and board in the village could be had at one dollar and seventy-five cents a week. Wood for a fire in the young girl's room was extra. By the way, girls were not spoken of then as they now are, the school being for young ladies. The letters give a picture of a decidedly earnest yet very agreeable daily life.

Dear Mother:

It is impossible for me to tell the exact number of our scholars but probably there are over two hundred. And although there are so many, and though the school is not yet completely organized, there is never at any time any confusion or noise. Miss Grant spends about half the morning in the schoolroom; Miss Lyon is always there during school hours, and there are eight or ten other teachers who devote the whole day to us. . . . All the regulations and rules have not as yet been proposed to us. The teachers are very strict with regard to all such rules as are adopted, but they manage us as a judicious husband manages his wife. They make us say for ourselves what we will do (which they see to it shall be just what they wish) then give us the credit of governing ourselves, and after all this is contrived, why to be sure we have no excuse if we don't do just so and so. . . . We go to school at eight in the morning and are obliged to be instantly in our seats. No communication at all is allowed during school hours. At twelve we are dismissed but must walk immediately home as fast as possible without running, never stop by the way one instant upon any occasion. At quarter past twelve we dine. At two every young lady must be at her seat again in the schoolroom. At quarter before five every young lady must return home with the same precipitation as in the morning to be ready for tea at five. The time after tea till seven may be devoted to visiting, walking, etc. . . . At quarter before nine all studies and writing must be put away and at quarter past we must, our lights being extinguished, be safe in bed.

The next letter is from a student in the same academy, and her correspondent is an elder brother who is deeply interested in her progress.

Dear Brother:

It is a matter of business about which I write this morning. I have chosen my subject for my composition, though I have not yet worded it. The idea it contains is this: Whether in this country it would be well that we should dispense with all such honorary titles as D. D., LL. D., Esq., Hon., etc. I do not know how I came to choose such a subject, but as I have chosen it I shall keep it. Now for my business. I want to see Burke's view (or whatever it is, I do not remember the name) of the French Revolution. I have a confused idea that the work, or Paine's answer to it, would throw some light upon my subject and render it less opaque for I can't see quite through it. . . . If you think it can do me any good I should like to have it. I do not imagine that the book would give me any light upon the subject directly before me, but I suppose that I might gain from it some general ideas upon the leveling principle. If you think I can and it would be practicable to transmit the book I should like to have it. I did not mean to say if it would be practicable. I should have said if it would be convenient. If not, why I suppose I can get along with a tolerable degree of comfort without it. . . . I wrote the foregoing yesterday. . . . Since that time I have been classed. Perhaps it may be a satisfaction to father and mother to know the fact that I am placed among the seniors and shall receive my diploma at the ensuing examination. The class contains only eleven. Eleven young ladies taken from among so many is a very small proportion. Many of the young ladies are (and begging Miss Grant's pardon I think they have good reason to be) a little disappointed that it is not larger.

If any reader of this book has a mother whose good fortune it was in her girlhood to attend the Passaic Seminary of Paterson, New Jersey, presided over by Miss Anna Rogers, whose assistants were her sisters Miss Elizabeth and Miss Jane, she may ask and be told something about the way in which a young ladies' seminary was opened in the morning. A generation later at least than that of Miss Grant, Miss Rogers maintained her school on the same basis. I can see her now with my eyes shut as she came floating into the room in her dress of lusterless and soundless black, with white frills at throat and wrists. We girls thought her quite old, but she must have been in the flush of early womanhood.

She gave us simple Bible expositions daily and supplemented them with talks on the conduct of life. Her predecessor in the scholastic line, Miss Grant, had her method which is described in a letter and extract of which I give.

> Monday. Went to the seminary at a quarter before nine. Miss Grant came in, wished the ladies a "good morning." They returned the compliment by rising. Miss Grant then enquired how many of the young ladies attended meeting the day before but omitted taking the texts and heads of the discourses, made some general remarks, then led in prayer, short. Questions on the twenty-second chapter of Genesis. We are studying Genesis in course. She usually gives us from ten to fifteen verses to commit to memory, when the lesson for the Sabbath is given out. . . . We were then requested to write the history of Shechem or Sychem, Hebron and Padan Aram. In writing the history of a place we first tell what country it is in, what part of the country and its situation relative to some other place, in what parts of the Bible it is spoken of, what remarkable occurrences took place there, etc., etc. After the Bible lesson the class in geometry were requested to take their seats in the chemical room and the others to arrange themselves in sections, to attend to arithmetic.

A girl of sixteen who understood so well the art of preparing a paper on a given subject and knew where to find her references had taken her initiative in that which, after all, is the chief end of school-going, in that she had learned how to study. Let us shift the kaleidoscope again.

Our other student writing to her mother asks assistance that a father must have been very proud to send.

Dear Mother:

At present I have a great deal of business on hand to accomplish before the close of the term. I have each day several classes to hear which require considerable of strength and time to sit about two hours in the schoolroom each morning, attending lectures, etc., about one hour in the afternoon to attend to the devotional exercises and the taking in of our accounts, and about one hour to periodicals; that is, to the reading of them and the reciting of interesting facts and items in the schoolroom. Besides, within a week or ten days, I have been requested to prepare a set of questions for the whole of the Political Class Book; not common questions which may be easily answered from the book, but certain whys and wherefores, and with regard to any incidental facts that may be brought in by the way. In short, they are to be made out of nothing, to be manufactured like the bricks in ancient Egypt, without straw. I hope that next summer, the young ladies will be much benefited by them.

Moreover, there is my composition for examination. It must be finished in a fortnight. I was told so yesterday. . . . We have but five weeks before us and I have not yet chosen my subject. . . . These examinations are attended by a great many people, therefore it is natural that I should feel a little anxiety. Miss Lyon is now delivering lectures upon the subject of benevolence, and Miss Grant upon the preservation of health. I hope I shall be able to improve by these many opportunities that I now enjoy for improving my character. . . . I wish, Mother, you would give my love to Father and ask him if he will please to write me soon and tell me about the political sentiments of Mr. Frelinghuysen and Mr. Grimke, and

> whether they have taken an active part about the Sabbath mail and Indians. I want also some of the Jackson arguments in justification of the conduct of the general government toward the Indians, and the reasons why it is thought that general government cannot interfere with the affairs of Georgia; and I also wish to know if there is anything to justify the late attack upon the missionaries in Georgia and their imprisonment. I have heard considerable said about this of late but only upon one side of the question. I suppose there is another side and I should like to hear it. As I am a representative of a Jackson family, though no Jacksonite myself, it is well enough for me to understand these disputed points.

The early maturity of these schoolgirls is somewhat in contrast with the later development of girls in preparatory schools at this date. Do girls change or is it that they are differently treated, that less is expected of them now and that they remain children longer than formerly they did. The insistence on the word lady is noticeable. Jane Austen's first novel bore on its title page the legend, "By A Lady." Behind her ladyhood the author veiled her personality. The young ladies of the early and middle nineteenth century were sought in marriage about the time of life that our young women are beginning their freshman year. Times change, and we change with them.

From the Ipswich Academy and the tutorship of Miss Zilpah Grant teachers went out to repeat her work in every state of the growing republic.

The sentiment of the school was so strongly and unaffectedly pious that its graduates sought service in missionary fields as a matter of course.

Miss Ward, to whom I am indebted for the information, states that in 1835, only seven years from the opening of her Ipswich school, thirteen missionaries of the American Board, fifty-three teachers in the West and South, and three hundred teachers in New England, New York, and New Jersey had gone from under Miss Grant's instruction.

Chapter III

A Liberal Education

THE DESIRE FOR a liberal education is almost universal on the part of young women. It is confined to no class and is as imperative and insistent in homes of deep poverty as in homes of wealth. There are young women whose childhood has been passed in crowded tenement homes, and who have been compelled to leave the public school at fourteen that they might aid in paying the rent and buying the clothing of their families. These girls toil voluntarily evening after evening in the winter season, studying advanced English, advanced German, or the higher mathematics, toil with a diligence and fidelity that are amazing and beyond praise. Why do they do it?

Usually because they are ambitious and wish to be prepared for better positions in business, but sometimes that they may gratify an insatiable hunger for learning. In provincial districts away from the beaten track, in simple homes of mountaineers, in mining towns, in the deep green country, there are daughters of poverty who keep before them throughout their early youth the hope of going to college. They teach little district schools, they work in cotton mills, they wait on guests in summer hotels, they work hard and long that they may save a sufficient sum for a beginning, and if able to enter college they toil early and late that they may pay their way. A year ago I sat in the room of a young girl, a brilliant student in a western college, and glanced at its simple furnishings, the books on its shelves, and the desk that had witnessed the persevering labor of its owner. The girl herself happened to be absent and the dean said to me, "Here is her photograph, the picture of a brave girl. She has earned her own support and paid her bills by her own labor since she was fifteen. She is twenty-one and she will be graduated next year."

Fathers and mothers, their heads growing gray, their shoulders bowed under heavy loads cheerfully abridge their comforts, cheerfully work harder and save more in order that they may send a gifted daughter to college and let her have the chance and the education on which her heart is set. They are in the middle of the road where the ruts are rough and the stones hurt tired feet, but they make light of their self-denials and say nothing about privations or loneliness if they may bestow on the child of their love the thing she craves.

In homes of wealth it is the same. Here the self-denials are less severely felt, although parents miss sorely and yearn eagerly for the presence of a daughter in the sweetest time of youth when she leaves them to be gone during the greater part of four years. They know full well that no other four years will ever be precisely like these in which they are sending their darling out of their sight. Still they utter no protest. In this age and country there is the conviction that every man owes his children all the learning they want, and that no parent is fair and just in his dealings with daughters if he fail to equip them thoroughly for the accidents, unforeseen events, and possible contingencies of an unknown future. It is not only that the man who is rich today may be poor tomorrow or the reverse; it is that we understand that a disciplined mind and trained powers are absolutely essential in the conduct of life whether the girl's coming empire shall be in her home or in the arena of conflict, whether she shall be wife and mother, business-woman or member of a profession she needs and must have a liberal education.

In the previous chapter we have seen that the accent in the earlier education was placed on ethical principles and moral development. The liberally educated woman was to be first of all an earnest Christian. If we have partially lost our bearing and drifted into the notion that education for women may be liberal without being Christian, it is time that we call a halt and recover something of the wisdom of those who went before us. I am not of those who fancy that colleges are perilous places for young women. Undoubtedly, there is danger in some quarters that girls who enter college in what may be termed a spiritually illiterate condition, who have had no Christian training at home and are not grounded in the faith, may leave college indifferent or hostile to religion. This is not the fault or the defect of the college; it is rather the fault and the defect of an imperfect home training. Instances are on record showing that girls have gone to college carrying with them a childlike faith, and have left it impressed with doubts and opposed to personal religion. These instances are offset by thousands of an opposite character, and in almost every case on inquiry it has been found that the seed planted in the home had been thrown by the wayside where the birds of the air were ready to pounce upon and devour it. Our daughters can hardly be liberally educated if the foundation stone of early religious nurture in the home has been omitted.

College training is eminently valuable to girls for several reasons. The first is that it broadens their horizon and greatly adds to the sum of their pleasures. It teaches them how to study. It increases their intellectual resources and gives them the indefinable thing known as culture.

They learn to be impersonal. A woman's primary impulse is to measure everything by the effect it has on herself. The thoroughly educated woman, the woman for whom college has done its best, looks not only upon her own things but also on the things of others. Her mind is a weapon plastic to her will.

If it is her purpose to teach, to study medicine, to enlist in the fields of art or journalism she receives her initial training in her alma mater. The teachers of the new generation are college-trained women. The student in the school of medicine has a college diploma. The girl who is fitted to take her place as the wife in the home of a man, educated as a man must be for politics, diplomacy, or business, needs an education similar to that of her husband. Lacking it, she will not be his congenial comrade and companion.

The second thing that a college education does for a student is to give her a certain balance. She learns to see life steadily and to see it whole, her perspective is truer, her sense of proportion is juster for the education she has received. If it is her great good fortune to be trained by professors who are more than learned men and women, who are more than versatile scholars, who are broad-minded, deep-hearted and large in the truest meaning of the words, she will carry through life the stamp of their individuality.

A third benefit conferred by a college upon its daughters is found in the fact that it groups together and keeps in a homogeneous life for a term of years girls from all sections of the country and almost from every quarter of the globe. The daughter of the ranch, the daughter of the prairie, the daughter of the metropolis sit in the same classroom.

The sweet-voiced southern girl, the emphatic westerner, the conservative New Englander, the cheery Californian, the courteous Philadelphian, the wide-awake New Yorker, the child of the manse, the child of the avenue palace, the child of the mountain farm meet in chapel, at table, on the campus, in recitations, in sports and each derives something desirable from all. Besides a process of elimination and polishing and mutual understanding, students at college cease to be dependent on mothers and sisters and acquire an amount of self-dependence that proves invaluable to them in maturity.

Among the most hopeful indications in this republic is the general interest in education and the fact that the woman graduate is not singular. With the second generation receiving a diploma on commencement day and the third having its name enrolled that in due time it may secure its quarters and belong to the alma mater of its ancestors, surprise, comment, and criticism are alike out of date. Our girls are in college just as they are in the public and private schools and few express the fear that college will do them harm or have any doubt about its doing them good. One sees dark-eyed Syrian girls, dainty maidens from Japan, daughters of China and India, and sometimes a girl from Oklahoma with the straight hair and high cheekbones of the red men among the students gathered today in American colleges.

For those who have not strength or time to spare, preparatory schools and boarding schools of a high character do as much as is done for their friends in college. Let it be added that the health rate of students in both schools and colleges is decidedly higher than that of girls who live a less regular life, and take less exercise out-of-doors. College students excel in athletics as they do in study. Basketball, tennis, golf, boating, driving, walking, mountain climbing, and whatever else has to do with a healthful outdoor life are theirs in full measure.

The objection has been made by those who hold that advanced education tends to unfit girls for home duties, to unsettle them, and to force them into unfair rivalries with men, that the colleges graduate students who have gained little by the curriculum. They point to a woman who is no doubt well mannered and amiable, but who has not acquired much real culture and who must be classed among those who are ordinary.

The woman's college although still new is not on trial in this regard. Colleges for men have sent forth their graduates for hundreds of years, and a large number of the men who have borne their endorsement have been well-meaning but commonplace fellows. Until every man graduated from an institution of learning towers like Saul head and shoulders above men who have not had his opportunities and advantages, it will be unfair to measure girls by this exacting standard.

In the last analysis for both men and women the result depends on the personal equation. It is the girl and not merely her education with which we are concerned. Given in the girl capacity, diligence, self-restraint, and strength, there is nothing that a liberal education will not do to make her the finest flower of the race.

Henry Ward Beecher used to say that a well-educated man would kindle a fire more creditably than an ignorant one. In the daily contacts of life, in the adjustments to situations, in the readiness for emergencies, the benefits due to intellectual discipline are constantly seen. Dr. Henry Churchill King, president of Oberlin College, wrote in reply to a letter of mine,

> I am sure it would be very far from true to say that any large proportion of our young women are preparing for professional work. I judge that, aside from teaching, very few are looking to such work. It has not been my judgment, in view of Oberlin's seventy years of experience, that a college education in any way unfits a girl for home life. We have always believed so thoroughly in the home here that I am sure our students have not gone out with any underestimation of the place of the home in life. And our graduates, both men and women, have certainly shown their readiness for altruistic service after graduation. The work of the Christian Associations seems to me to have been quite influential in this direction in late years, but this spirit has been marked all along.

Oberlin as a coeducational institution has made its deep and ineffaceable impression on the nation, and its magnificent record is an open page that all may read.

A testimony as interesting and as pertinent as that of President King was sent me last autumn by Mary E. Woolley, president of Mount Holyoke College. Miss Woolley says,

> While a large proportion of our students at Mount Holyoke prepare for professional life, very many of them remain at home and I should like to say most emphatically that I think a college training does not unfit them for domesticity. The tendency is toward altruistic work, that is, as I understand it, the attitude which considers others rather than one's self, but I am sure that I do not know where that sentiment is more needed than in the home. I fear that this is something of a hobby of mine, and that I could discourse at too great length concerning it, for I feel so keenly the injustice of the criticism that college training unfits a girl for home life. I am confident that that view is not borne out by the facts in the case.

Similar expressions have reached me from other educators and perhaps I may best epitomize them in concrete form by quoting the words of a woman whose service has been given for many years in the Chair of English Literature in one of our most progressive colleges, "Of one thing I am certain: the republic of women has taken no harm!"

If as it sometimes happens a girl returns from her four delightfully stimulating years at college to find home life for a while insipid and dull, if another girl is restless and dissatisfied and does not immediately succeed in fitting herself into the right niche, if once in a great while a girl's superior education leads her to look with patronage on home-people who are provincial and untaught, these exceptions do not interfere with the rule that applies to the majority. In such instances the original defect is in the stuff of which the girl was composed. Youth is a period of ferment at the best, and transient dissatisfaction seldom works permanent injury. Dr. Lavender, in a story of Margaret

Deland's, remarks in conversation with a friend, "I never grudge a little unhappiness to the young." Underneath the light raillery of the wise old doctor there lies a profound truth. We are not the worse for a bit of discontent here and there if we make it a stepping stone to better things. After an interval most college women do as their sisters have always done; they adapt themselves to the situation and take hold of the day's work. Where that day's work may be is not their concern because we all go where we are sent. The chief consolation is that good work is never lost, and "whether we serve in the Lowlands or the Highlands, we get a soldier's pay."

Dr. King's allusion to the work of the Christian Associations confirms the opinion of those who have watched with growing satisfaction the deepening hold of association work on student life. The Young Women's Christian Association in the college takes the newcomer by the hand in her freshman year, introduces her at once to congenial friends, affords her an opportunity for Christian companionship, prayer, and Bible study, encourages her to worship in the church of her own denomination, and surrounds her with an atmosphere of Christian fellowship and Christian faith. The association has the support of the faculty in the colleges where it exists and in some institutions where its initiative was accepted merely with toleration, the Christian Association is now regarded as "a vitalizing influence," and is upheld with enthusiasm. The daughter who goes from a Christian home to college and who is without delay numbered among the members of the Women's Christian Association at work therein, will never be in danger from the miasma and the chill of doubt. Nor will she take a lower rank in her classes as a student than others who have drifted from their safe moorings.

Chapter IV

The Cheer of the Unattained

A GIRL FRIEND wrote one day to an older woman, frankly telling her a bit of experience. "All my life, until I was grown," she said, "the one thing I most wanted, and never could get, was a piano. Other girls had pianos and did not seem to care for them, but my soul was full of tunes that wove themselves in and out of my thoughts, and my fingers thrilled with the wish to fly over the keyboard. But we could not afford a piano, and I had to be contented without it. My childhood passed, and my teens, and when I was a year or two beyond twenty, a change in circumstances enabled me to gratify my longing. I now have a beautiful piano, of fine tone and compass, and I am taking lessons, but, alas! my progress is fearfully slow. I appear to have no talent, when I thought I had genius. I shall never be a musician and the piano stands before me, a bitter mockery!"

The mistake made by this young girl was twofold. In the first place she was demanding the impossible. Every art requires apprenticeship. The mason does not lay bricks, nor the carpenter floors, until he has been taught how to handle trowel and hammer. The dressmaker and the milliner and the tailor have to acquire their skill at the cost of painstaking effort persisted in during a period of careful training, and practiced thereafter for months and years. When the artist paints a picture, there is more in it than inspiration or a love of beauty. Long hours of study and arduous toil have made the hand able to interpret what the eye saw, and the brain composed. Youthful writers make the same mistake when they fancy that their stories and essays are fit for publication merely because they have found enjoyment in writing them, and have an absorbing wish for a literary career.

Every art and profession exacts hard and strenuous work before the highest proficiency can be reached, and music is perhaps the most jealously exacting of all the arts. Not months but years of study and practice are requisite if one would be a skillful performer on an instrument and it is very doubtful whether ease and grace, flexibility, and fine technique can be gained in a great degree by a pupil who begins when childhood is past.

The second mistake was of a subtler kind. Why regard as a mockery that which is as yet unattained? In very truth it is the unattained which gives zest to the commonplace and brims the cup of our daily life with keenest joy. The music asleep under the black and white keys may not answer to the touch of the unskilled player today or tomorrow, but it is there and in some happy hour a response may come. Half the worth of living is in trying to advance. So long as there is a goal in front of one, so long as one may try to achieve, the will should be braced, the student should gird on her armor, and the endeavor to succeed should be the salt and savor of the day's work. No artist ever fully reaches the heights of his attainment in this world. There will be something to strive for in the next life.

Tennyson puts a great fact in his poem, "Wages":

Glory of warrior glory of orator, glory of song,
Paid with a voice flying by to be lost on an endless sea—
Glory of virtue, to fight, to struggle, to right the wrong—

Nay, but she aimed not at glory, no lover of glory she;
Give her the glory of going on, and still to be.

Browning in "Rabbi Ben Ezra" strikes a brave note for those who are toiling but have not yet seen results.

Then welcome each rebuff,
That turns earth's smoothness rough,
Each sting that bids, not sit, nor stand, but go!
Be our joys three-part pain,
Strive and hold cheap the strain,
Learn, nor account the pang, dare, never grudge the throe.

Once in a while, in a confidential moment, your mother or your aunt may let you have a glimpse into some secret of her soul that you never suspected. Would you believe that your quiet little mother who is so contented with her housework and her ministry to the dear ones, who spends a whole sunny afternoon patching the knees of her small boy's trousers or turning a faded garment that it may enter on a second service has always longed for a broader life, has had visions of crossing the Atlantic, visiting picture galleries, standing in great cathedrals, and seeing vista after vista open and unfold in Swiss mountains? She has never said much about these dreams of hers, but sometimes her hand trembles a little when she closes a book of travel, and sometimes in her own room with the door shut she sighs over the things that for her will probably never be more than unfulfilled wishes. Yet she is, whether or not you comprehend it now, a more interesting companion, a more successful mother, and a dearer friend to her boys and girls than she could be if she had no longing beyond her own door. It is the literal and prosaic mind that undertakes drudgery and finds in it no relief. Drudgery that goes on and on without a thought to gild it is the routine of the treadmill. Drudgery that sees something to be gained beyond, that is lighted by imagination, carries with it a certain freedom.

The mother in the moment when she lifts the curtain lets the daughter see that all her life she has been a saint, perhaps a poet, while she has been baking bread and making beds and saving money to send her daughter to college.

Far up among the New Hampshire hills I once met a woman to whom life had been a series of privations and to whom hardships were the daily bread of existence. I sat with her in her kitchen and saw how wonderfully she accomplished large results with little means. Her days began before dawn, and she was the last one to seek her pillow at night. She wore a print gown and a blue-checked apron, her hair was gray and fastened in a little knot at the back of her head, her hands were knotted and toil-worn. But I loved to talk with her and I learned to know that she had sounded the depths of a philosophy so rich, so profound, that her sisters might well sit at her feet. One day she took me up a winding stair into what she called her tower room. Before we went, she took off the blue-checked apron and put on a spotless white one and folded over her bosom a thin white kerchief in which she looked like a picture of her Puritan ancestress.

"Now I am ready," she said brightly. "I never let anyone whom I do not love go with me upstairs to my little nook under the roof."

It was a small place, but it had three windows with seats around them and there were a rocking chair, a table, and a bookshelf. I looked in amazement at the books. Here was a worn copy of *Whittier*, here were *Emerson's Essays*, a *Life of Andrew Fuller*, and a Bible that had been read over and over many and many a day. My friend smiled as she saw my surprise and then waving her hand at the prospect outside she said, "I could never have lived comfortably with other people but for my sunsets. When I was a girl I taught in the little school that you can see down there at the turn of the road. Then I had ambitions. I wanted a liberal education. I wanted to know books and men, but I married and we have been poor, and I have never gone very far from home." She added with a kindling eye, "Whittier says for me what I have never been able to say for myself.

" 'I know not what the future hath
Of marvel or surprise;
I only know that life or death
His mercy underlies.

" 'I know not where His islands lift
Their fronded palms in air;
I only know I cannot drift
Beyond His love and care.' "

After a while we closed the door of the tower room, and went back to the kitchen. The husband and sons returned from the fields. A string of cows came slowly home to be milked. The mother sifted flour and made biscuits for supper. I understood how it was that the homely tasks had not worn her out and that her soul was so regal. I understood, too, something of the pretty fancy that made her dress in white when she entered her tower room. I knew how it was that she could be so patient when things were untoward, and why it was that circumstances had never crushed her spirit. She had in her life the blessed cheer of the unattained.

Just suppose, girls, for a single minute that you already had in your possession everything that your heart craves. You would have no desires left. I can imagine nothing less tolerable than to own everything one could see. It is far better, is it not, to have something to strive for?

The richest man on earth has no monopoly of sea and sky, and the poorest may enjoy his neighbors' beautiful lawns and gardens without responsibility or care.

Robert Louis Stevenson in a lyric called "A Song of the Road" strikes the note I mean.

The gauger walked with willing foot,
And I the gauger played the flute.
And what should Master Gauger play
But Over the Hills and Far Away.

Whene'er I buckle on my pack
And foot it gaily in the track,
Oh, pleasant gauger, long since dead,
I hear you fluting on ahead.

The same master of thought and verse makes a picture for us in "The House Beautiful" that is worth looking at when we are a bit discouraged with things about us.

A naked house, a naked moor,
A shivering pool before the door,
A garden bare of flowers and fruit
And poplars at the garden foot:
Such is the place that I live in,
Bleak without and bare within.

Yet shall your ragged moor receive
The incomparable pomp of eve,
And the cold glories of the dawn
Behind your shivering trees be drawn;
And when the wind from place to place
Doth the unmoored cloud-galleons chase,
Your garden gloom and gleam again,
With leaping sun, with glancing rain.
Here shall the wizard moon ascend
The heavens, in the crimson end
Of day's declining splendor; here
The army of the stars appear.
The neighbor hollows dry or wet,
Spring shall with tender flowers beset;
And oft the morning muser see
Larks rising from the broomy lea,
And every fairy wheel and thread
Of cobweb dew-bediamonded.
When daisies go, shall winter time

Silver the simple grass with rime;
Autumnal frosts enchant the pool
And make the cart-ruts beautiful;
And when snow-bright the moor expands,
How shall your children clap their hands!
To make this earth, our hermitage,
A cheerful and a changeful page,
God's bright and intricate device
Of days and seasons doth suffice.

A great deal of inspiration to effort and endeavor is in the thought of the goal before us. We have not reached it yet but we are pressing on. Dr. William R. Richards in a very suggestive New Year's meditation tells us about a youth who was competing in an athletic contest:

> Three or four years ago over twenty thousand excited people watched a lad running full speed the length of a field. The papers the next morning were full of his praises, because he had made this great run successfully. Reading the accounts, I found myself curious to know how the boy himself felt when he was doing it; and meeting him some months later, I asked him how he had felt, or whether he could remember how he felt, when he was making that famous run. He told me he remembered very distinctly; he said that the only sound he was conscious of while he was running down the field—where really those twenty thousand excited people were filling the air with indescribable clamor—the only sound this boy was conscious of was the quick footsteps of the runner behind him, who was trying to overtake him. He said the impulse was almost irresistible to turn his head and see whether this other man was gaining; but then the thought flashed through his mind of another great race, run a few months earlier in England, where the leader did glance over his shoulder and it had lost him the race; and so my friend had kept his face straightforward and won. A runner running to win in a close race must not waste time looking back over his shoulder.

In this race of life that we are running we must not be depressed or discouraged if we do not immediately win. There are prizes that will never be ours here.

We must wait for them. Turn to Saint Paul's Epistle to the Philippians and read the message he sent to his friends. It is a message, girls, for you and me.

> Not that I have already obtained, or am already made perfect; but I press on, if so be that I may lay hold on that for which also I was laid hold on by Jesus Christ. Brethren, I count not myself yet to have laid hold: but one thing I do, forgetting the things which are behind, and stretching forward to the things which are before, I press on towards the goal unto the prize of the high calling of God in Christ Jesus.

It is in the pressing toward the goal that the finest, sweetest, and highest satisfactions of life are found. So far from regarding with discouragement a study, a trade, or a vocation in which one does not immediately succeed, the incentive should be in the struggle itself. There is a good deal of mountain climbing which seems to be nothing but hard work. Presently, however, the climber comes to a turn of the road where he sees a beautiful prospect before him.

A woman whose years were almost at the meridian had longed just as had this girl of whom we have been talking, to gratify her love of music. At fifty she began taking lessons. She never learned to play very well but she said, "I am learning to understand music I hear better than I once did, and my lessons will help me to know what the angels mean when I listen to their harps in heaven."

She had put her hand on the edge of a happy secret. Hers it was to know the alphabet of the cheer that lies in the unattained.

Chapter V

Health and Beauty

IN THE PAGES OF the novelists from Sir Walter Scott to William Black, from the author of *Evelina* to Thomas Hardy, beauty is the prerogative of youth. A significant token of modern progress is found in the changing ideal of beauty as one period passes and another comes. The earlier writers take for granted a certain fragility and delicacy in young women, and do not expect that highborn damsels shall have the rude vigor reserved by them for buxom dairy maids. Yet Sir Walter endows Jeannie Deans with an amount of sturdy health and of endurance that would be enviable in any age, and on occasion the women who are his favorites do not shrink from peril and privation only to be borne by the aid of perfect health.

Thomas Hardy in that loveliest of his creations, *Bathsheba Everdene*, shows us a girl who could ride or walk with grace that made it a delight to watch her, a woman whose energy was tireless and who could carry forward her plans without fear of interference from nerves or sick headache, and William Black fairly revels when his steady hand draws pictures of girls who are not afraid to climb the hills, face the breezes on a mountain lake, or stand on the deck of a yacht that is flying before a stiff gale.

Health and beauty are united in the types familiar to us on the pages of romance, and at least by inference they are mated in the dreams of the poets.

To go back to Homer and the breath of the morning we do not associate even transient illness with Helen of Troy. Shakespeare's women are usually well. Tennyson indeed allowed the exquisite Elaine to fade away and die of her hopeless love, but on the other hand he shows us the fair Enid on the march walking over rough places and smooth at the bidding of the wrathful Geraint, mile after mile in a relentless tramp that would sorely tax the muscles of a twentieth-century college girl.

To go to a source unique in interest, our English Bible, we there discover instances of health and beauty in combination in the peerless Sarah, the gentle Rebekah, and the radiant Ruth of the Old Testament, to say nothing of Rachel, Abigail, and Esther. In Solomon's magnificent epitome of the ideal woman given in the last chapter of Proverbs, he lays out a program so full and complete that only a woman in the finest health could possibly undertake it and summing up he says, "Strength and honor are her clothing."

Let us put in our minds the especial accent on strength.

It is a matter for congratulation that in our conception of beauty in girlhood we do not omit health and strength. It is an added reason for congratulation that we are today a little less insistent than we were a decade ago on mere athletic prowess. There is something between the attenuated lady with long ringlets and a taper waist, who embellished the annuals of our grandmothers' time, and the golf and tennis champion with sun-browned cheeks and arms and a general air of hoyden clinging to her skirts. A beautiful girl should have about her nothing mannish. The feminine ideal is not incompatible with unbroken health, robust strength, and the infinitely appealing grace so charming in girlhood.

If one of you should ask me to name the foundations of health and beauty I would without hesitation tell you that they are built on plenty of sleep, plenty of exercise, plenty of good food, and plenty of fresh air. I use the word plenty with intention. If our girls are to be beautiful and to be well they cannot be scantily supplied with the essentials of wholesome life. Pale cheeks and haggard eyes follow on a meager allowance of sleep. This is one reason among others why all things considered a girl often returns from a year of hard work at school or college in a condition of exuberant vitality which her sister at home has failed to achieve. When lights must be out and students in bed at ten o'clock they are sure of two hours sound sleep before midnight and a subsequent portion of uninterrupted slumber until the rising bell in the morning. Our working girls lose more than they dream in this regard because they are so fond of prolonging their evenings either in amusement or in housework and sewing, while rising early they seldom get a sufficient allowance of sleep.

Brain and body are made over by the nightly rest and without it no girl can long retain the freshness of her youthful looks. Food should be abundant and plain if girls would keep the spotless skin and the clear eyes that all admire. In the wake of rich pastries and surfeiting sweets arrive unsightly blotches and disfiguring pimples.

Exercise in the open air, let the weather be what it may, is imperative for girls if they would keep well. No young girl should be aware of disordered nerves, or be subject to the tyranny of frequent headaches. As for backache she should not so much as know the alphabet of its torture. A physician said to an enquirer who asked him if she might safely venture out on a damp and misty day, "Any weather conditions out-of-doors, let them be what they will, are better for those who would be well, than indoor conditions can possibly be. Live in the open if you want to be well."

To exercise beyond one's strength may be unwise, but daily exercise of some sort in the fresh air is indispensable to health. Sunlight is better than twilight, but if a girl is engaged all day in a shop or factory, a schoolroom or office, let her not forego her walk under the stars. We are apt to succumb to the American temptation and to dwell in overheated houses. Lack of ventilation and excessive heat from furnaces or a steam plant rob us of vital force and make us languid and irritable. When a girl shivers in a room on a winter day unless the temperature climb to the eighties, she is paving the way for grip and pneumonia. Girls who would be habitually well should avoid the use of drugs, stimulants, and narcotics. Cold water freely used and fruit which is nature's remedy for most maladies will keep a girl free from the attacks of insidious disease. One who is in fairly good health and not in the state known as run-down, is generally immune from contagion, although an epidemic may be stalking through the community.

Habitual health is at once a preventive and a defense in the matter of disease. The modern girl hardly needs it and yet she will pardon a suggestion about daily bathing. A bath from head to foot every morning of one's life should be a rule similar to that famous one of the Medes and Persians which was never abrogated. Merely to wash the face and hands is the makeshift of indolence. The body is covered with a fine network of skin like the most delicate lace. If this network becomes clogged the skin does not do its work of throwing off impurities.

An eminent physician writing to girls on this subject answers the question, Shall I take a cold or a warm bath? in the following manner: "This will depend entirely upon the constitution. Take the bath that makes you feel strongest and that takes the least vitality from you. Unless there are reasons for not doing so a daily bath of some kind is an absolute necessity for good health. There can be only an arbitrary distinction between hot and cold baths, but a convenient way of classing them is this: a hot bath means over ninety-eight degrees Fahrenheit; warm is between ninety and ninety-eight degrees; tepid varies between sixty-five and eighty degrees; and a cold bath is any temperature below sixty-five degrees."

The same authority adds that the effects of a bath are to be cleansing, stimulating, and soothing; that a warm bath should be taken at least once a week, and that a cold sponge may be used with advantage by most girls every day.

Girls sometimes inquire whether or not soap may be used on the face. As the complexion is exposed to wind and dust, fine particles of the latter will sift into it and remain as a disfigurement unless at least once a day the face is washed with either fine almond meal or a delicate toilet soap. The best time for this process is at night, just before retiring. Make a creamy lather and rub it well into the skin with the tips of the fingers, afterward removing the soap by a thorough rinsing.

A young girl who is careful about this washing every night will seldom complain that she has blackheads or blotches on her face. After a bath there should be brisk rubbing with a rough towel to insure circulation. Cold feet and hands indicate deficient vitality, but a hot feverish hand is as little to be desired as it shows a tendency to the same end or to a mournful waste of tissue. A cool, firm hand, warm feet, and a cool head betoken high health.

Do not undervalue the beatific influence of sunshine. A sunny room is in itself sanitary. Do not undervalue either the necessity to rest when you are tired. Healthy fatigue is not a thing of which to be ashamed, and if one is tired one should go by herself, sit quietly down or stretch out at full length on a lounge or divan for a brief rest. From five minutes to fifteen spent in this way now and then will prove wonderfully recuperative if one is weary.

Recognizing the necessity of rest for weary workers, many factory owners are providing restrooms where their operatives at the lunch hour may secure the short rest that will better fit them for the afternoon's toil. There are few articles in daily use from our gloves and stockings, our shoes and hats, to the food that comes to us in tins and the preserves that are sealed in glass jars, from the dainty perfume in a cut glass bottle on my lady's toilet table to the fragrant cake of soap in its tinted wrapper, from the books we read to the stuffs we wear and the pins that fasten our clothing or hold fast our hats that have not been under the deft hands of some woman or girl. A million young women go forth in the gray dawn of winter and the sparkling dews of summer to spend days in monotonous toil. The problem for them of maintaining health and beauty is far more difficult to solve than it is for Lynda and Harriet, whose lives are comparatively sheltered and luxurious.

The toiler can do it if she is willing to take time and pains, to sacrifice nonessentials, and to avail herself of whatever ameliorating conditions come in her way. The Young Women's Christian Associations, not alone of this country but of the wide world, are aiming to provide social centers for the working girl where her health may be concerned; opportunities of rest may be afforded her, and some chance given for her life to expand like a flower instead of close up like a frost-blighted bud.

To the girls who are not compelled by stern circumstances to toil late and early I would give this reminder: Labor is by no means an unmixed evil nor is drudgery to be dreaded. In fact unless one has work of some sort to do, work that is felt to be worthwhile and therefore ennobling, one will wither and fade as early as if compelled to toil too strenuously. Daily work tends to health; indolence and its resultant ennui are foes to health. A girl whose days drag on in the monotony of nothing to do is almost as badly off as her sister whose days wear on in the monotony of too much to do.

Life loses its savor if it is spent in idle drifting.

Ask a man how he would feel if he passed day after day in holiday leisure. If the morning brought no anticipated task and the evening no conviction of work well done, he would probably tell you that he simply could not stand so empty a life. One of the conditions on which we hold in fee our birthright of beauty and our birthright of health is the strict fulfillment of the day's work.

I shall never forget a summer day spent some years ago with Celia Thaxter at her home on the Isles of Shoals. She had a garden where flowers rioted, blooming as they do where the sunshine and the sea gave them continual baptism. Mrs. Thaxter stood in her garden with the June light falling on her head, crowned with its glory of silver hair, the great knot fastened at the back and thrust through with a silver arrow. She wore a dress of silver gray with opalescent shiftings. Her beautiful face in its comely middle age had parted with none of the witchery of girlhood. The lines of her figure were graceful and she might have been painted as a goddess of the sea. Her house was full of flowers. Her personality was strong, sweet, and intensely womanly. Such health and such beauty may be given to us in girlhood and maintained through a long life if we do our work well, live in God's open air and His glorious sunshine, and trust Him with childlike faith for all the unknown future. Worry eats into beauty and ravages health and it is a heartbreaking thing to see a young girl fall beneath its say. My last word about this is the word of our Savior, "Consider the lilies how they grow; they toil not neither do they spin. And yet I say unto you that Solomon in all his glory was not arrayed like one of these."

Chapter VI

The Dreamy Girl

A MOMENT COMES in girlhood when the eyes are less occupied with the practical realities about them than with dreams and visions of enchantment. The young girl has her reserves and her innate reticence and often her nearest and dearest do not so much as lift a tiny edge of the curtain that drops between her and them. They speak of realities, prosaic affairs of the marketplace and of the present, while for her the true realities wear opal tints and are wreathed in violet mists. She is like a child who looks from the farmhouse door at the range of hills that rims the landscape, wondering what may lie on the other side.

A girl at this time leads a sort of dual life. She is busy with her books or her sewing, she is helping her mother or hearing her brother recite his lessons for tomorrow, while in the back of her mind there are thoughts of what she is going to do and of castles in Spain that cast no reflection visibly on the surface of the day.

It would greatly surprise some parents and teachers could they take a peek into the busy brain of a demure little maid, who is all attention to their desires and fails in no duty while yet she is carrying on a mystic life of her own. Long before she knows anything about love and lovers this girl has her poetic fancies and weaves them around some hero who exists only in an ideal world. Of this type was Elaine, living with her old father and rough brothers in a half-ruined baronial hall, ready to give her whole heart to Lancelot because her maiden dreams had been so sweet and so full of wistful longing and worship.

Such a maiden Tennyson describes when he says, "Her eyes are homes of silent prayer."

A girl of this special type does not tell anyone, sister, mother, or chum, what she is thinking about. She would find it hard to put her thoughts into words and a blush would creep over her cheek at the mere hint of disclosing them to anyone in words. She is like the bud, closely folded and holding its fragrant secrets under lock and key.

Clara Laughlin in the *Evolution of a Girl's Ideal* has given a glimpse of what may be going on in a girl's mind all unsuspected, while to her mother and her friends she is still a child. She tries to make herself look as old as she can. She timidly and from afar pays homage at the shrine of a gallant youth, who never so much as sees her. There are elderly women who have not forgotten their early days and they well remember the pangs with which they saw a similar idol of their dreams marrying an ordinary girl whom they considered most unfit for so lofty an honor.

But girlish dreams are by no means entirely of love. An ambitious girl has her dreams of fame. In days that are past her ideal poet was Mrs. Hemans, a lyric poet of rare sweetness if not of great originality. The schoolgirl of other days read Mrs. Hemans and decided that she, too, would write verse and have her niche in the temple of literature. In these days she makes an idol it may be of Kipling or of Mrs. Humphrey Ward, and has hopes her poetry and her story shall be in every magazine.

Elizabeth Browning knowing full well the heart of the dreaming girl is for all time the favorite poet of girlhood.

Among our own writers Elizabeth Stuart Phelps perhaps touches most intimately and most truly the heart of a girl, though in *Rebecca*, Kate Douglass Wiggin showed a keen insight that was very convincing.

A woman who has achieved an enviable place in letters told me that when she was a girl she had her dreams of fame and with the greatest care that her work should not be discovered, she spent several years in writing a book. Her home had a garret of the old-fashioned amplitude with shadowy corners and an eastern window where the sun peeked in at dawn, while on the other side there was an outlook to the golden sunset. The girl's room was at the foot of the stairway that led to the attic, and she kept her sheets of foolscap in an old trunk in one of the attic corners. Sometimes in the early morning and oftener in the late afternoon she flitted silently upstairs and in the solitude of the garret pursued her engrossing task. She wrote and wrote. Finally after many sheets of foolscap had been covered her book was done. The next step was to find a publisher. She made her package up as neatly as she could and under cover of night, escorted by a faithful maid who would have gone for her through any adventure, she went to the express office. She was dressed for the enterprise in an old cloak belonging to the maid and on her head she put a cap such as old peasant women used to wear, a cap with a wide white frill, which must have looked quaint and queer around her youthful face. She was sure that the clerk in the express office, a lad who knew her brother, had not the faintest idea who she was and when after some weeks her story came back it was so addressed that no one at home knew anything about her disappointment. Since then she has written many books but into none of them were woven so many dreams as into that first child of her fancy.

On the whole it is the girl who thinks she can write and who cherishes a hope that she may one day become a successful author, whose dreams are the pleasantest. They fill her with hopes and joys that are exquisite while they last, and although her dreams may never come true they do her little harm. If they send her for inspiration to the fountains of literature, if they lead her to thoughtful reading of great books, and if they yield her mental enrichment and help her to a wider vocabulary, they do her much good.

Still another dreamy girl has visions of setting the world right. She sees a good deal to criticize. She longs to relieve poverty and suffering. This girl does not care for little things that lie within her reach; it does not occur to her to amuse the baby while the baby's mother goes for a walk, or to mend a pair of gloves for her father, or enlist her brother in an indoor game so that he may spend a safe evening at home instead of a profitless one outside. Her dreams are of being a settlement worker, a philanthropist or a missionary, and unless she sees a probability of becoming one of these she does very little at home. The dreams that have to do with possible great deeds, while obscure and trifling things at hand are neglected, belong to the realm of folly.

The idlest girl I ever knew and the one most given to daydreams was a girl whom I shall call Miranda. She was a pretty maid with a peach-blossom face and hair that held golden lights in its wavy masses. Her favorite seat was a rocking chair; her favorite occupation novel reading, and her favorite solace a box of chocolate creams. Established in a sunny window with a cat purring at her feet, Miranda would spend hours while other people were busy. Contrary to the predictions of all her acquaintances she woke from her absorption after a while and took hold of life with energy and decision, but it was not until the rude hand of misfortune had shaken her out of her ease that the stronger stuff of her character made itself apparent.

A Danish poet has a picturesque ballad about a damsel whom the neighbors called Briar-Rose. She was a willful bit of a lassie who danced and sang the livelong day, who never wove or spun or helped her mother in the household, and the village women shook their heads and sighed over her idle life. But one day a great freshet came, and it was Briar-Rose who by an act of heroic presence of mind saved the village from destruction, though she lost her life in the effort.

Girls, the chief danger to avoid in dreaming is the danger of drifting. "Life is real, life is earnest." Unless we have motive and purpose, unless our lives tell for something, we are in peril of losing some precious opportunity. This is the hour of opportunity. What yours may be or what mine in the day that is coming, who can tell? But we must be ready for it and fill the hour with action and with whatever can do most for our neighbor and for our homes.

To serve the present age is a duty we may not shirk.

Occasionally a dreamy girl cultivates as if it were admirable a sort of absentminded indifference to what is going on about her. Wrapped in her own thoughts as a mantle, she takes little note of reality and though her attitude may be a pose it is exceedingly absurd to those who observe her. This peculiar affectation belongs to girls who are very young; as they grow in maturity they throw it off and are a little impatient with the phase if they happen to see it in somebody else.

To be absentminded if the infirmity be real is a misfortune and by no means an evidence of genius. We cannot afford to go around with our head in the clouds while our feet are on the ground.

Nevertheless, we must not underrate the dreamers. Behind every good deed done there is a thought, and this thought was in someone's mind before the deed grew into being. The people who dream are very often the people who see, and dreaming and seeing precede doing. No gift so glorious has been bestowed on us here below as imagination. It comes freighted with power and majesty straight from heaven and lifts us from the clouds and makes us like the angels. One who has little imagination never rises into the bright regions that are held in fee by the dreamer of dreams. The dreamy girl though she dwell in the plainest cabin on a mountainside, though she wear homespun and perform every variety of drudgery, is superior in the privileges that belong to the soul and may take a higher place than the princess robed in satin and living in a palace, who is literal, matter-of-fact, and drearily prosaic.

The great explorers, the great discoverers, the great inventors have been the dreamers, and though it is not woman's province to shine in these lines, in her domain of home and love she is most benignant and most blessed to whom come day by day the dreams that make life's commonplaces radiant.

My dreaming girl if I know her has a bookshelf in her room and on it are the books she loves; among them Shakespeare and Tennyson, a fairy story or two, a volume of essays, and one or two romances that are faintly penciled here and there on the margin of the pages. A girl's books reveal something of her inner life. If on a table under the shelf there is a Bible, not for show but for daily use, and perhaps *Faber's Hymns* or *George Herbert* or the *Christian Year*, there is evidence that the dreams are pure and sometimes bear the dreamer up as on ethereal wings.

Opening the well-worn volume of Tennyson that is often in the girl's hand, a leaf turned down testifies that she in her degree as the great poet in his has found pleasure in following the gleam.

Not of the sunlight,
Not of the moonlight,
Not of the starlight!
O young Mariner,
Down to the haven,

Call your companions,
Launch your vessel,
And crowd your canvas,
And, ere it vanishes
Over the margin,
After it, follow it,
Follow The Gleam.

Chapter VII

An Even Mind

"I AM EITHER ON the crest of the wave or in the trough of the sea," said a girl complacently as she came tripping into the room and seated herself on a divan, resting her head against a cushion.

"Today I am on the top wave; tomorrow I may be fathoms deep in despondency."

"You speak," I answered, "as if your sudden fluctuations of mood were beyond your power to control, almost as if they were to be matters of congratulation. You are in the crescendo movement of your life this morning, and the diminuendo I take it is to be expected in due season. My dear child, you have my compassion. I wish I could endow you with what an ancient sage thought the greatest of boons: an even mind." The little lady only laughed, being rather proud of her moodiness which she thought a badge of genius. Moods and tenses are among those properties that must be reckoned with in our estimate of values. We are born with tendencies and temperaments that have much to do with our usefulness and our ability to live comfortably with other people. There are women who never learn how to adjust their moods to the moods of their friends. In my girlhood I knew two young women each of whom as compelled to live in a home not her own. One was so cheery, so genial, so ready to lend a hand and so even in the tenor of her ways that everyone counted it a pleasure to have her as a guest. She taught a little school and she had not much money; she was plain of feature and somewhat awkward and clumsy in appearance, but no one gave these trifles a thought. She herself was such a sunbeam.

One day there was a question in a household where she had been tarrying as to whether she could be accommodated there during the coming winter. The house was small and the family large, the mother somewhat overburdened. It seemed as if the little teacher must go in quest of a boarding place somewhere else. Up piped a little voice and a lisping child decided the affair in his own way. "There is room enough," he said in broken baby talk, "for dear Miss Susie," and Miss Susie continued where she was, taking stitches for people, filling up chinks, singing snatches of gay melody, and bringing an element of vitality indoors as often as she entered.

The other young woman had more money, had traveled, and had enjoyed the benefits of society and culture to a degree unknown to Miss Susie. But she was the victim of chronic melancholy. The fiend of discontent clutched her in his grasp and a habitual frown settled on her brow. A face that nature had meant to be attractive was disfigured by a scowling expression and her voice was discordant and rasping because it was keyed to a perpetual murmur. Nobody wanted Miss Hetty and when on occasion relatives felt compelled to give her asylum they did it without pleasure and were openly relieved when her visits were completed.

I saw nothing of this unfortunate victim of the low mood for many years and had forgotten all about her when one day I happened to meet on a journey a person who bore her name. It was an unusual name and in conversation I learned that the man came from her native town. After a while, still forgetting that I might be on dangerous ground, I observed, "I used to know your cousin Hetty."

"Did you indeed," was the reply. "My poor cousin Hetty! She was the most difficult and perverse human being I ever saw or heard of, and though she was my own cousin I never had the least patience with her. Somehow or other Hetty was warped in the making. I often wonder if she is contented in heaven."

Mother Goose exclaims: "Mary, Mary, quite contrary / How does your garden grow?" When I have the misfortune to encounter a Mary who is contrary I feel like asking her how she expects anything to grow in the garden of her heart when she shuts out so much of the sunshine it ought to have. Be it noted that people abandoned to moods are much oftener in the lower mood than in the higher. If of sanguine temperament and by the way of seeing what they wish in rose-color, they have their days of brightness and they might be pardoned if these were in excess of the opposite variety. Alas! Those who are easily elevated to a height are too often as easily plunged to a corresponding depth. Life has its exaltations and its eclipses. Of them I am not speaking.

You will have your red-letter days, so jubilant, so triumphant, that they will stamp themselves on memory forever and be kept as royal anniversaries. You will have, very likely, your days of sorrow when you sit under the cloud and feel that never again can you be the same, in the missing and mourning a dear one. I am talking to you about the common days, the days that are marked by nothing special and are simply filled with little tasks, little duties, ordinary studies, errands down the street, calls upon neighbors, hours in the kitchen, hours in the living room with the family, hours in solitude; just common days. When from Monday until Saturday there is no excitement, no anticipation beyond the accustomed routine, what we require is an even mind. If we suffer ourselves to be domineered over by a mood of passion, of anger, of petulance, or of depression we shall be unfit for the duties of the common days and we shall find it increasingly difficult to overcome the losses occasioned by our wasted powers and our apathy and inertia.

Some of us attribute quite too much importance to states of emotion. Constantly one hears the complaint, I do not feel as I ought, especially when the subject is some aspect of what we call the religious life. Properly looked at there should be no distinction between our secular and our sacred life. Religion is the binding of the heart to God, and all our days should be bound to Him and therefore all our lives should be lives of piety. We are not Christians on the Sabbath and pagans on Monday and Saturday. If we are Christians at all we are Christians always. Those who are honestly seeking to know something of the divine life and who have made up their minds to be servants and friends of Christ complain that they are not sorry enough for sin and not sensible of enough love for the Master they are following. Our Lord understands human infirmities. He knows that temperaments differ, that some have vivid imaginations, and some are very literal and matter-of-fact, and that for the latter heights of feeling are not to be looked for. It matters very little about our feeling in the line of duty, so long as we are careful to do right to the measure of our opportunity. Waiting for just the mood we long to have ends in disappointment and failure. The mood does not come and the moment of opportunity passes away.

The troubles which are most paralyzing when we concede too much to moods are very apt not to be real ones. Girls ought to be happy. They are in that bewitching time when trouble should not touch them when there should be the sweetness and radiance of a spring day all about them. If I may judge from letters written by girls widely separated as to locality and social station, the low mood is one of their most frequent trials. Girls struggle with the intangible. Phantom ills threaten them. They are a little impatient with inevitable delays. If they have no assurance that something they want will be theirs in a week or a month, they rashly conclude that it will never come to them and are correspondingly disturbed in consequence.

You may regard it as an exaggeration of statement but I am inclined to place low spirits in the same catalog with crimes. True, the person who is wading in a slough of despond and suffering from an attack of the blues does not steal her neighbor's purse or use profane language or speak falsely of a friend or covet what does not belong to her. She is not guilty of theft, deceit, malice, or blasphemy. Instead, she is wearing an air of resignation, bearing herself like a martyr, sitting wrapped in a gray fog, sulking and pouting and is robbing everyone in her home of tranquillity and peace. She is deliberately or thoughtlessly eclipsing the gaiety of her home. If she persists in yielding to the blues, she may drift into a state of nervous exhaustion and soon be a fit candidate for a sanitarium. If the blues become chronic and she entertain a fixed idea of grievance or disaster or even of some subtle offense she fancies she has committed, she may lose her reason.

The folly and danger of yielding to moods and caprices has never been depicted more strongly than in a book that recently provoked much discussion. Lady Kitty Bristol in the *Marriage of William Ashe* never attempted to control her moods. Whatever they were she became their sport: sometimes wildly mirthful, sometimes vehemently angry, sometimes utterly cast down. Never once in the story of her tempestuous career do we find the spoiled beauty endeavoring to control or restrain the mood of the moment, and her career found its consummation in a tragedy.

Solomon said, "Better is he that ruleth his spirit than he that taketh a city."

The effort for us should be in the direction of self-control. Not that we should be lethargic or insensitive or unresponsive to emotion, but that we should hold our emotions in check, guide them and not let them guide us, would be the true wisdom. Of course the buoyant nature, the nature that rides on the top wave and has its home on the crest, is the one that most of us envy. In the days of perfect health and strength, when we are occupied in tasks that we love and our friends are all around us, buoyancy is the outcome of conditions that have known no shadow. How to be brave and buoyant when things are awry is the puzzle for those who have not learned the secret of poise and of an even mind.

Nine girls in every ten are too much given to introspection; they are always pulling themselves up by the roots, they are scrutinizing their motives, examining into the springs of their conduct and looking too eagerly at their own souls. The tenth girl thinks very little about herself, devotes her silent periods to reading her Bible and praying to her Savior, and the rest of the time she goes faithfully about her work without considering why she does it or what effect she is producing on those around her. In other words she leads a normal and healthful life in which there is no margin for introspection.

Other girls have too much leisure on their hands. If they are in society and are gradually making the discovery that nothing is so profitless as a life spent in a round of diversion, they drift into dullness and ennui and complain of the tedium of society. The life of a butterfly may grow as wearisome as the life of a bee if it have no helpful intervals. The giddy round must pall if one be not so shallow that a meaningless life can content her. Satan finds some mischief for idle hands to do and the mischief that he finds oftenest is the domination of a sullen, ill-tempered, or fretful mood.

I hold that for most of us, for you and for me, the only

safety is in ignoring our moods and doing our work. Some work there must be for each of us, or we shall one day awaken to bewail the fallow fields that have lain uncultivated too long.

One of our temptations is to scorn the tasks that are obscure. We are convinced that we are fit for grand and noble enterprises but our day's work is humble and at the end of the week we have nothing to show except rooms swept and dusted, old people cheered, children entertained, sick people soothed, and trifling things done. We have not gone beyond our own doors, our own vineyard in a little spot that not even passers-by can see. But if it is our vineyard and the Master has bidden us care for and cultivate it, why should we be disturbed?

I do not know who wrote the exquisite lyric which I insert here for you.

Perhaps you have heard of the message strange,
Of violin makers in distant lands,
Who, by breaking and mending with skillful hands,
Make instruments having a wider range
Than ever was possible for them, so long
As they were new, unshattered, and strong.

Have you ever thought when the heart was sad,
When the days seem dark and the nights unending,
That the broken heart, by the Father's mending,
Was made through sorrow a helper glad,
Whose service should lighten more and more
The weary one's burdens as never before?

Then take this simple lesson to heart
When sorrows crowd, and you cannot sing:
To the truth of the Father's goodness cling;
Believe that the sorrow is only a part
Of the wondrous plan that gives through pain
The power to sing more glad refrain.

Chapter VIII

Our Restless Girls

ALLUSION has been made to the restlessness of girlhood. It is widespread and confined to no class or clique. Country girls beat against the bars of their cage with as much impatience of restraint and intolerance of limitations as if they were wild birds caught in a snare. City girls look about them and scorning the ease and leisure of home life find their opportunity in the business world with an eager zest that amazes veteran toilers. A girl joyfully leaves a home of luxury to sit all day long in an office behind a clicking typewriter that she may have her share in the larger life of the world and be released from the obligation to entertain, to pay visits, and to flit through society in a mere butterfly life.

Another girl having spent a term of years in regular and strenuous study very naturally asks herself to what purpose it was done if she may not use what she has gained as her brother does without objection from anyone. Were John after graduation to sit down contentedly to crochet work and embroidery, to pouring tea for afternoon callers, to driving in the park and dancing in the evening he would be regarded as an indolent and shiftless person of whom little could be expected, and who was discrediting to his family.

Why should Jane, her brother's peer in the classroom, equipped as fully as he for industrial or professional vocations be compelled to waste her young energy and her mental strength in profitless idleness simply because of her sex? Girls not infrequently leave college with a question like this burning into their souls, insisting upon an answer.

These are not days when sensible girls are crying for careers. They do not want a career, they care little for excitement or acclamation, and they know to a fraction the market value of that ephemeral quality known as fame. They do want to test their mettle to discover where they can be of most use and what they can do to the greatest advantage. It is not that the restless girl sets too low a valuation on her home or on society, but that she yearns for life in the open and for the opportunity either to earn her livelihood or to help others by wage-earning, or in still another field to aid her struggling brothers and sisters by unselfish effort and endeavor.

The restlessness is not peculiar, as I have said, to the girls of one locality or one variety of training. Everywhere girlhood reminds one of plants pushing sturdily toward the sun and throwing out shoots in the direction of upward progress. The girl on the east side of New York, foreign born herself or the child of parents who still speak imperfect English, is as restless and eager after a few years in the public schools, as resolute in her determination to exchange a lower kind of work for a higher as is the daughter of a multimillionaire trained from the cradle for society and born to the purple. Everywhere girlhood is restless and it behooves us to accept the restlessness not as a symptom of disease but as a hopeful sign for the coming womanhood. Stagnation is death. Living waters have their rejoicing or complaining murmur.

Before we condemn a girl for girding against the monotony of the home, before we censure her for seeking a wider sphere of action than her native village affords, shall we not at least try to be perfectly fair? In my judgment home is the most beatific, the most satisfying, and the most inviting sphere a woman, young or old, can ever find. Yet thousands and thousands of women can have a home only by paying for it the price of their daily labor. Very few girls going forth to any occupation do so from merely selfish motives. The money they earn aids in the support of the family, in educating younger sisters and brothers, and in making provision for the maintenance of kindred who would else be shorn of many comforts. When this is not the case and the girl feels within her a strong impulse to undertake her share in the world's work, why should she be denied?

The severest criticisms are frequently bestowed on young women who dedicate their time, talents, and education to the noblest and most unselfish work open to man or woman, the work of the foreign missionary. Can Ellen find nothing to do at home that she must go to China and be in danger of martyrdom, or to India or Japan, Arabia or Africa, to teach women and children and to read the Bible in zenanas or palm-thatched huts? Why should she forsake her mother who is growing old that she may carry the gospel to a distant land? If Ellen instead of becoming a foreign missionary were to marry and following the fortunes of her husband go to the remotest corner of the globe, not a word of deprecation would be said.

Not so very long ago a cloud of prejudice hung around every girl who undertook the study and practice of medicine. Little by little that cloud has cleared away and the woman doctor, a familiar figure, is recognized, trusted, and honored, whenever she appears.

But for the restlessness of the pioneers who braved insult and obloquy and endured hardness, doctors would still be of one sex only. It seemed in a beginning not yet far removed that a woman could not study medicine without putting herself beyond the pale of womanhood.

Not to multiply instances, the restlessness of woman has

been at the source of many of the most beneficent philanthropies. A woman goes as an angel of mercy to the prisons of this land, sits down in the cell and points to a star of hope when the prison gates shall open and the convict come forth. Women on the battlefield and in the hospital minister to the wounded and the fevered, and women go from door to door among the very poor carrying blessing and comfort to those who are almost in despair. The helping hands of womanhood in this world of ours are the unresting hands of the restless, who cannot be satisfied until they are employed.

Girlhood is a period of ferment and effervescence; often there is difficulty in adjustment. The girl does not readily discover the work she is best fitted for. For example, in an inland village a young woman was teaching a primary school. She understood the requirements of the grade and filled the situation acceptably to her townspeople, the school board, and the children. But she was not at ease. She did not enjoy teaching and she felt that she was doing with half-heartedness what someone else could do better with a whole heart. She wrote to a relative in a city and asked for a business position under him. Rather under protest he granted her request. To his surprise she displayed uncommon administrative ability and capacity and to make a long story short, she is at the head today, after five years of training, of a business that nets her a generous annual profit and in which she oversees hundreds of operatives.

People speak loosely of society girls as if they were necessarily a class by themselves, and necessarily idlers. In reality the life of a young woman after she has been presented to her mother's friends and is eligible to whatever society has to offer is anything but idle. She is extremely busy. From one day to another in the season her hours are preempted and the round of amusements and entertainments is no less fatiguing than would be the engagements of business life. It is most unjust to the daughters of opulence, whose lives are supposed to be devoted to pleasure, to take for granted that they have not their own restlessness. It is a wholesome restlessness and it finds its satisfaction in many forms of service to those less fortunate than they.

Not long ago I spent an evening in a crowded chapel where night after night circles of King's daughters assembled, and large audiences of working girls wearied with standing at the loom or behind the counter came together for a social evening. An exquisite young girl with the air of a princess stepped on the platform and sang as only one could whose magnificent voice had had the training of the best masters. This girl, a favorite in society, came two evenings a week to sing for her sisters and to teach them singing. Another girl charming in face, low-toned and sweet in voice, gathered about her every week groups of little girls to whom she taught sewing. Yet another, who has the world at her feet, devotes a number of hours weekly in settlement work, sometimes teaching English literature to hungry learners, sometimes telling the sweet story of old to those whom she is fain to guide to the feet of the Master.

Those who ignore the fact that a girl may live in society and take her part in it with sweetness, courtesy, and savoir faire and yet at the same time adorn the Christian profession in all sincerity, have looked through blurred glasses.

Still and always she chooses the better part who prefers quiet ways and finds her best opportunity in ministries of love to the home dear ones. Home is the best background. An exquisite girl, the flower of an ancient race, and the only daughter in a large household said musingly, "There are a great many things I'd like to do, but the Lord's will seems to be that I shall be just a daughter at home. I cannot be spared to go anywhere else while there are so many good people coming and going, aunts and uncles and cousins, and kin of all degrees; while my father needs me at night to play for him, and my mother in the morning wants me to help her keep house, and the servants in the kitchen cannot get on without my help here and there."

Blessings on her! She is filling her niche as fully and as honorably as if she were writing for magazines or singing to listening thousands or healing the sick or keeping books in a merchant's office.

Once we have found out where duty lies and accepted it, there is an end of discontent. Even what may be called divine discontent ceases when the Lord's will is understood and accepted.

Shall we not say with Miss Waring:

I would not have the restless will
That hurries to and fro,
Seeking for some great thing to do,
Or secret thing to know;
I would be treated as a child,
And guided where I go.

Wherever in the world I am,
In whatsoe'er estate,
I have a fellowship with hearts
To keep and cultivate,
And a work of lowly love to do,
For the Lord on whom I wait.

So I ask Thee for the daily strength
To none that ask denied,
And a mind to blend with outward life,
While keeping at Thy side;
Content to fill a little space,
If Thou be glorified.

And if some things I do not ask,
In my cup of blessing be,
I would have my spirit filled the more
With grateful love to Thee,—
More careful, not to serve Thee much,
But to please Thee perfectly.

Chapter IX

About Signing Your Name

DID YOU EVER give a thought to the history of names? Few subjects of study are more fascinating, and few reach back so far and so deeply into the very roots of language. Surnames enfold in themselves the story of the race, and to those who have looked into the matter they reveal secrets of the past with an unerring precision akin to divination. Christian names, too, are interesting, each of them having its lovely meaning flashing like a gem and setting the wearer apart from the hosts of other people living at the time.

Whatever the name may be, whether bestowed upon you in memory of an ancestress or given from caprice because those who selected it thought it beautiful and worthy, it is not the least valuable possession that you must carry to the end of your days. If you are Mary in your cradle you will be Mary when your hair is white, and as Mary you will do your allotted work through the years of your life. No one can rob you of your Christian name. You may be robbed of gold or lands, you may lose friends, you may lose health and hope, but through everything your name will be the distinguishing feature which presents you to the world you know. For this reason let us talk a little about the commonplace topic of signing a name.

I have spent so many precious minutes in efforts to decipher the names of correspondents with whose penmanship I was not familiar, that I write with great earnestness on this subject of the signature.

Your name signed at the end of a letter or appended to a contract or other business document stands for yourself and represents you in the eyes of the world. Your world may be a little one but it is yours. Entirely without your cooperation your world may enlarge and touch the worlds of others so that the name you sign today on a bit of paper may in some strange and unexpected manner affect interests and people of whom you at present are in ignorance.

A letter is the most imperishable thing on earth. One writes it in haste and sends it off and forgets all about it. The recipient takes no special care to save it from destruction and yet years after the transaction has been forgotten the letter crops up in an old box or an attic, and is read by those for whom it was never intended. A lady a few days ago received from an old school friend a letter written by herself a half century earlier. It was of no particular importance, except as an illustration of the indestructibility of things once written. Every year the press issues volumes of memoirs largely composed of letters sent from hand to hand in the days before the railway system was invented, when letters were carried by king's messengers with relays of post horses at different stations on the road. There have been revolutions and changes: empires, republics, and kingdoms have been radically altered in the course of time. Fires have devastated cities, cyclones have leveled towns in the dust, and yet a yellow letter in faded handwriting survives every crash and partakes of immortality. When you see this you must acknowledge that letters belong to the serious affairs of life and that they should be properly signed by their writers.

I hope none of you grow so weary by the time you finish a

letter that you let your signature trail off in a blind fashion that it takes an expert to decipher. The signature should be the clearest and most obvious part of a letter, with character and distinction and legibility, and not with the peculiarities of a puzzle.

One's Christian name is not permissible as a signature except in letters addressed to one's immediate family. One's pet name should be used only in the same exclusive circle. To your father and mother, brothers and sisters, and your adoring grandparents, you may be Betty or Fanny or Sue, but to others you must adopt a greater formality and sign yourself Susan, Frances, or Elizabeth. Outside the family circle be careful to write your name with both Christian and surname, and taste of the time be it noted, is a little against the use of middle initials. Unless you have established a habit in this line, my advice is that you send your full name to everyone. If, however, people are accustomed to seeing your name written with a middle initial, a change might prove confusing and seem to savor of affectation.

Your name on a check or receipt should never vary. Write it as you have been accustomed to do without so much as the slightest variation. When you are introduced in a bank in which you wish to open an account, your signature will be at once a safeguard to the bank and yourself. You will be expected to write it in your ordinary way, and it will be accepted as your legal signature.

The usage of an earlier day allowed women to sign their names with diminutives in an informality now condemned. Thus it has happened in several instances known to me that women approaching fourscore years are legally known as Nellie, Molly, and Janey instead of as Eleanor, Mary, and Jane, and their abbreviated names appear in this way in contracts and the like. The catalog of girls' schools in your mother's day included Angies, Peggies, and Flossies. Look over the latest catalogs of the foremost girls' schools, issued in the present century and you will find in evidence Florence, Margaret, and Angeline. Little toddlers of two and three are addressed as Beatrice, Prudence, and Phyllis, and perhaps it is just as well since absurdities such as Pet and Sis, Daisy and Pearl, Birdie and Baby have a way of clinging and are ridiculous when their wearer is a tall young woman in the charmed region between eighteen and twenty.

A neglected branch of education, as women too often find to their regret, is acquaintance with the common forms of business. Fathers in their chivalrous affection for daughters are far too ready to treat them as if they were children at an age when responsibility may at any time, perhaps suddenly, be laid on youthful shoulders. For this reason among others it is well that after the age of twelve every girl who can do so should persuade her father to give her a monthly allowance large enough to cover most of her personal needs. At eighteen or twenty a young girl may have her own bank account, with bank book for deposits and checkbook for the payment of bills. The safest way to pay accounts is by check because every check honored by a bank is a voucher that a certain sum of money has been paid. Large city banks do not care to be bothered with small accounts kept by schoolgirls, but in the suburbs banks are more accommodating and do not refuse the trouble of caring for small monthly deposits. You may never become rich as the world counts riches but if you have a sufficient income to meet your ordinary wants and leave you ever so slight a margin, you will be an independent person who need not envy the woman of wealth. All business connected with banks whether for savings or simply for business purposes must be carried on in an exact and systematic manner, and you must remember that you are accountable for whatever your signature stands for.

Bearing this in mind you will learn never to sign your name to any paper, contract, or document which you have not read and with the terms of which you are not satisfied. Girls and older women, too, often say, I have entire confidence in Brother Tom, Cousin Ralph, or Doctor Will, a lifelong friend of my family. It implies no lack of confidence carefully to read any paper presented you by a relative or friend before you append to it your signature.

In writing to strangers, remember that although it is the extreme of vulgarity to sign yourself Miss Smith or Miss Putman and that the accepted usage is Barbara Putman and Phe Smith, still Miss should be inserted in brackets at the left hand of your signature. How else shall a stranger know whom to address when replying to your letter? If he answers your letter addressing you as Mrs. Barbara Putman his letter may go to the widowed aunt for whom you are named. Invariably when writing to strangers a woman should take pains to indicate whether she is married or single, and if married she should of course put her husband's name in the part written in brackets. Thus Phe Smith might be Mrs. Alexander Smith. There is no exception to the rule compelling a woman, married or single, to sign herself by her name no matter to whom she may write but the Miss or Mrs. should never be forgotten unless she is writing to intimate friends and kinfolk. It should never form a portion of the signature but be separately indicated. Very likely a girl will find herself a member of a club or committee, an official board or a governing body in her college or Christian Association. The rules as to signatures given in reference to business are imperative in committee and club work.

I am almost afraid while talking on this matter of signing one's name to suggest to girls the propriety of making a will. Many older people shrink from this duty, partly because they do not like to be reminded of death and partly because they have very little to leave behind them. But every girl has keepsakes and trinkets, books she prizes, articles of furniture on which she sets a value, and personal belongings that are dear to her. Sometimes they are heirlooms and sometimes she has saved her money little by little at the cost of self-denial that she may buy an article, a picture, a curio, or a rug on which she had set her heart. A keepsake book in which one writes from time to time what disposition she would like made of her treasures in case of her death will not hasten that event. But it may on some coming day save trouble to those she loves, and convey a touching and tender pleasure to one who sees how dearly she was loved. You will best prepare yourself for the larger responsibilities that may come to you later by being very neat and orderly in the management of your present small affairs.

Any girl who is a wage earner, and many girls today are self-supporting, knows to a penny the extent of her resources. She knows how much she earns and just what she ought to do with it. A college student away from home and perhaps preparing to become a professional worker has her stipulated allowance, or else if she is working her way she has the sums she can make. In this case, too, she knows what she ought to spend and how much she ought to lay aside. Along comes to either of these girls a persuasive person who has wares to sell. His wares may be furniture for a room, or books for a library, or they may consist of other things calculated to woo and win the feminine heart. He offers on the payment of a small sum to place the entire library, set of furniture, or whatnot in the girl's possession; the remainder is to be paid in smaller or larger amounts at stated intervals. As the owner of the goods must charge a percentage for credit, and as a girl may not always find herself in funds to settle the cash payment when due, she may discover to her distress that she is in the fetters of an uncomfortable indebtedness. Before signing her name to a contract of this kind, a girl should be very sure that her income will neither fluctuate nor become interrupted or nonexistent before she has completed her payments. As few can be absolutely certain on the latter point, girls are wiser not to involve themselves in entanglements of this kind. They are good investments only for people who have no reason to fear the termination of a steady income. Wait for the piano, the sewing machine, the typewriter, or the set of coveted volumes until you can pay for them at the moment. This will prove the more economical procedure, as one always has to pay for the privilege of credit.

A girl at school became enraptured with the charms of a very delicate and beautiful evening dress worn by a richer girl. The first girl knew that her father could not afford to let her pay fifty dollars for a simple frock of white muslin with insertions and embroideries, and the air given by a fashionable dressmaker; her wardrobe was made at home by her mother, and cost little as compared to that of her friend across the corridor. About this time a prize of fifty dollars was offered by a friend of the school to the student who should write the best essay on a selected theme. Our little country girl was successful in composition and rushed to the conclusion that she would secure the prize if she tried for it. On the strength of her anticipation she sent an order and her measures to the town dressmaker, accompanied by a letter of introduction from her friend. On the day that the gown came home with the bill the prize was announced in the competition, and it was not awarded to the buyer of the beautiful gown, but to somebody else. Imagine if you can, her dismay and discomfiture. In an agony of tears she rushed to the room of her favorite teacher and confided the whole story to her, saying, "What shall I do?"

"Tell your father all about it," said the teacher.

"I can never do that," the girl replied. "Father works so hard. It mortifies me to think of making his burdens heavier by my folly."

"Tell your father," again said the teacher. "He will understand and will help you."

That night she wrote a long letter and sent it home, and by return mail the daughter received a remittance of fifty dollars and not a single reproachful word. But her conscience urged her to another confession, and she wrote the whole truth to the dressmaker who very kindly relieved her of the gown so that she was able to return the money unbroken to her father.

If this little true story has a moral, it is this: Never order anything by mail or otherwise on the chance that when the bill comes in you will have the means to pay the cost. Be sure on this point before you sign your name and incur a business obligation.

Never sign your name in any connection of which you may in days of better judgment be ashamed. This advice applies to letters of all kinds; to letters particularly of sentiment, of enthusiastic friendship, and to letters written in a mood of anger or resentment. Your name, as I have already said, stands for yourself. Do not send it anywhere unless you are sure that you will be happy to meet it again. In all circumstances sign it clearly so that it may be easily read.

Chapter X

Love's Dawn

WHEN EDITH comes shyly in at twilight, takes a seat beside my fire, and half turns her face away as if she has something to say and still does not know how to begin, I bide my time. I have probably noticed a change in Edith during the last month or two, and have occasionally observed the young doctor, who has lately taken the practice of the one who went away to assume the duties of a professor elsewhere, in rather close attendance upon her. The new doctor seems a straightforward fellow, manly and capable, one likely to rise and to win his way, and it has been a pleasure to watch him going about and making friends.

Edith is a dear girl and usually has a train of admirers. We all supposed a year ago that she would marry the new minister, but it transpired that he was engaged when he came to us and that his fiancée was a college mate of Edith's, which explained the fact that he called oftener upon her than on any other girl in the parish. Up to this time Edith has been heart-whole. I am not sure, nor is she, whether or not she is still heart-whole, though it is suspected that the doctor is in love with her.

Girls often imagine themselves in love when they do not so much as understand the slightest outer edge of the deep meaning of this great passion. Love is like fire, a dangerous thing to play with, although the best of friends and the most loyal of servants when rightly handled. Love is like the wind, which may bring life to the lungs and health on its wings or may go tearing through the universe with the devastation of a cyclone. Love is like the gold in the mine, well worth seeking, yet sometimes needing purification that its dross may be eliminated.

Love turns all the wheels of human industry, is the motive power under the world's machinery, makes worthwhile every enterprise on the earth, is coequal with life, outlasts death, and reaches onward into heaven.

What does my golden-haired Edith as yet know about this mightiest of forces?

The truth is that girls at least are much oftener in love with being loved than with the man who loves them. They like to be sought, to be singled out from the crowd, to have the devotion and adoration that are freely poured at their feet by the man or men who strive to be their faithful knights. Occasionally there is a girl like Elaine who dies of her love for Lancelot, he having no love to give her. Fortunately Elaines are few and far between. Sometimes there is a girl who is like one in a story written by Alice Brown and called "The Grass-Green Maid." This foolish child fell easily in love with the suitor who came urging his plea, and hurried to tell him that she could not live without his favor; whereupon in several cases he turned and went away, leaving her disconsolate. An unasked admission of love, real or fancied, is usually fatal if made by a girl to a man. It is man's province to woo, and woman's province to be won.

"I found myself," said a girl one day, "anxiously asking Will to come in, and I checked myself at once. Why should I let any man think that I cared very much whether he called or said good-bye at the door?" How I wish that all girls had this wisdom. Edith does not lack it. She will never be so stupid and so foolish as to let her doctor dream that his coming on a certain evening or his staying away makes very much difference to her. She will meet him cordially, enter with interest into his plans and listen when he tells her about his days, his drives, his cases, or whatnot. If he is tired and asks her to play, she will sit at the piano and let her fingers draw from the keys the music of Chopin or Mendelssohn. If he is hungry and tired, she may give him a chafing dish supper but she will by no means monopolize him or entertain him often without at least the intermittent presence of the family, nor will she manifest regret when he takes leave. Should the doctor happen to be absent a week or two, and should Edith incidentally hear that during this time he has been calling at the house of her Cousin Fanny who has visitors from town, she will not express, and I hope she will not feel, surprise or annoyance at the occurrence. If there is one thing more than another that a man dislikes during the early days of courtship it is being bound by a too visible fetter. And, on the other hand, if there is one thing more than another likely to pique his interest it is indifference on the part of the girl on whom he is calling.

Should Cleon, who has been attentive to Phyllis, stay away from her for six consecutive weeks, following as many weeks when he had appeared regularly at her father's door twice or thrice between Sundays, it behooves Phyllis on his return to make no comment. Should he clumsily venture to apologize she will be wise to say lightly, "Has it been so long? Time does fly, and I have been so busy that I had not supposed it more than a few days since you called."

Of course, if a girl cannot say this truthfully she must keep silent, but on no account should she flatter a youth who is probably already sufficiently aware of his own value in the market by letting him suppose that he had been missed and mourned.

Lest you may imagine that I am speaking in a general way on this point, let me tell you that girls all over this country and Canada and from places beyond seas, have covered reams of paper and wasted bottles of ink in telling me how their love affairs have gone awry because of two things. The first, the fact that they did not know their own minds and were only in love with love; and the second, that they too openly bewailed the defection of men who also did not know their own minds and were in love with themselves.

A girl will tell me in ten breathless pages how for months together a certain youth offered her his homage, how she was sure she did not love him enough to accept the gift of his heart and hand, and how she finally refused him. Upon this, being a sensible person, the lover turned away, possibly left the place or continuing there, transferred his affection to a friend. "I now find that I have made a mistake," exclaims the young woman. "I did love John all the while, but I did not know it. How shall I get him back?"

In most instances the break is final. In nine instances out of ten, were the young man so weak, so brainless, and so wanting in self-respect that he returned to the fickle maid, the same drama would be enacted. She would again discover that she did not know what love meant and he would find if she accepted him that he had not drawn a prize. The girl who condescends to the interrogation, How shall I win back the lover who has departed? shows herself alike lacking in penetration and in dignity.

The number of marriageable young men in most of the older cities and towns is much smaller than the number of marriageable girls. In New England and the Middle States there are villages in plenty where the condition of things is similar to that in Cranford; an Arcadian simplicity prevails. Society is composed almost exclusively of women younger and older. There are not many men and young men are particularly in the minority. At army posts and naval stations girls are more fortunate. The gallant defenders of our flag are always ready to treat girlhood with the devotion that beauty and grace inspire. This is equally the case in newer localities where men are in the majority and women are few. In mining towns and on remote ranches the advent of a young woman is hailed with joy. Possibly for the reason that there are more eligible girls than men, the latter often act as though they were at a premium, and bear themselves with a kind of disdainful arrogance as though they felt that they had only to hold out the golden scepter and some sweet maid would at once advance and clutch it.

Until a girl has been suitably courted and has given herself in generous surrender to the man who has gained her love, his attitude should be that of uncertain supplicant and not of the assured victor. But while girls are so ready to show themselves delighted if a man singles them for favor, it is not surprising that the roles of both are a little confused. A man should never be too certain that he can obtain what he desires when the prize is a girl's pure heart and the yielding to him of her name and future.

Edith sits by my fire. After a while she says softly, "How I wish I could be sure that I am ready to leave home and father and mother, and give myself away for all time."

"Has it come to that so soon?" I ask. "The doctor has not lost his opportunities. Do you love him, child?"

"That's what I do not know," Edith answers frankly. "I am sure though that he loves me and I respect him. I know that he is good and I believe that I can help him. I think we can help one another. Father and mother both approve. It hurts me a little that they should be so ready to give me up, but then I would not have to go so very far away."

"Child," I reply severely, "if you love a man you ought to be willing to leave father and mother and go with him to the ends of the earth, to Greenland or Korea or the Cape of Good Hope. Geography should be nothing. If you love a man and if he loves you, you should find the Garden of Eden anywhere with him that he and you may choose on the face of the habitable globe."

"I have noticed before," says Edith, "that no people are so romantic as people with white hair. You are a dear, and that is why I am telling you first of all before anyone else knows it that I am really and truly an engaged girl, engaged to the doctor. I am going to live in the house on the corner, a stone's throw from my old home and I feel a hundred years older than I did last night, as if a great gulf were presently to stretch between me and my childhood."

Edith was right. I sometimes think that the only sentimentalists left are the men and women who have left youth behind them. And it is everlastingly true that love while it is the great uniter is also the great divider. When Edith said, "Yes," she took a step that separated her for all time from her past, with its happy ties; and that still by a strange paradox made that past more sacred than before. The girl who has known in its height and depth what true and loyal love is, the love that is willing to give all that it has, that is willing to forget self and crown with joy the life of another is thenceforward blessed among women. She is no longer merely in love with love. She is loving a man who has a right to be her true knight and servant as long as life shall last.

Chapter XI

Wooing and Winning

BOTH GIRLS and men are far too ready thoughtlessly to form associations and enter into relations that may permanently affect life. John meets Mary at a summer resort, an inn among the mountains or on the shore, and is impressed at once by her beauty and grace. The tricky god with the bow and arrows, who is forever meddling in the affairs of youth, sends a shaft straight to the young man's heart. His own sisters are as pretty, as clever, as dainty, and as bewitching as this girl who he has met for the first time, and who rises upon his vision like a newly discovered star.

Mary had brought a trunk full of clothes in the latest fashion to wear during her outing. Her immaculate shirtwaists, crisp stocks, modish skirts, and exquisite evening toilettes do their share in bewitching the youth, who thinks that a being so elegant externally must be as charming as she looks. Sometimes she is. Sometimes she is not. Occasionally, when an impulsive wooer loses his heart to a maid of whose people, training, and traditions he is entirely ignorant there is a brief season of enchantment and a long and dreary aftermath of disillusion. Mrs. Stowe wrote a story entitled *Pink and White Tyranny*, in which she gave a realistic picture of a marriage of this kind, a marriage that fettered a noble man to a brainless coquette and ruined his whole life.

In George Eliot's incomparable *Middlemarch* there is a similar example in the marriage of Tertius Lydgate, a brilliant and ambitious young physician, with a shallow and heartless girl, whose only claim upon attention was a slight veneer of social good form and a superficial acquaintance with music. There is nothing more bitter in the realm of fiction than the quiet remark of Lydgate years after his disappointing marriage had brought forth its Dead Sea fruit. He called Rosamond Vincy his basil plant, and the basil plant in fable flourished on the brains of murdered men.

I have known more than one wreck of this kind due to the headlong and impetuous lovemaking of a man who had been captivated by the merest outside attractiveness of a beautiful girl. Asking a man who had gained great distinction in his profession and who had arrived at deserved eminence by long and hard study and labor why he devoted himself a whole evening to a certain girl, neglecting others who were far more interesting, he frankly told me, "It is a liberal education to gaze at anyone whose face is so perfect."

"But she has not a sensible thought in her silly head," I answered.

"That is of no consequence. She satisfies my artistic sense of proportion."

Such a conclusion might do for a single evening but it would be most unsatisfactory for a lifetime.

I seem to be holding a brief for John, but indeed I am thinking even about Mary. A man has always a great deal more plus his household life than a woman has. Her limitations, those born with her and which accompany her throughout life, are not to be ignored. Her peculiar sphere of service must always be within four walls. If she is discontented, disappointed and unhappy at home, the reflex action upon all within it will make for continual wretchedness. If Mary knowing little more of John than she learns while voyaging across the Atlantic or meeting him at a house party in the Berkshires rashly pledges herself to become his wife, she may find that she has ventured the most precious things she possesses and lost more than she has gained. There are exceptions to every rule. People fall in love at first sight, marry in haste and do not repent at leisure. But considering that marriage is sacramental, that in every marriage service the vows are taken for life with the solemn words "until death us do part," it is only reasonable that as much care and thought should be bestowed here as are exacted in making other investments. In questions of business and property, sensible men and women act with forethought, look at the transaction from every point of view, and do not hesitate to seek and accept advice. Why should it be otherwise in a question so far reaching as that of love and marriage?

In the older countries parents and friends are consulted more generally than is the custom with us in decisions that affect the well-being of future generations. In France, Holland, England, Germany, and Italy mothers and fathers anticipate the coming day and make provision for their daughters in the matter of a dowry, and when the time for marriage arrives among the well-to-do, settlements are made which insure the wife's safety from want should reverses come. Ours being a new country we have not adopted this policy to any extent. Yet it is a wise one. Among other defenses against disaster, something in the way of financial security for wife and children takes no mean place.

I am saying nothing against love at first sight. If it be love and not a flitting fancy, not something due to mere propinquity or to the accident of circumstances, it will abide the wear and tear of time. That which is genuine may be trusted to endure strain and stress. But whatever may be said for John, Mary is sometimes fickle too. Shall I tell you of a girl I knew who was engaged to one of the noblest and truest of men, a girl who seemed in every way worthy of a man's fullest confidence and most loyal trust? They had plighted their troth with the entire approval and warm congratulations of a wide circle of friends. They were soon to be married. Suddenly, business complications and the death of a relative compelled the man to leave home for a distant post in the mining regions of one of our newer states. He begged the girl to go with him as his wife but her parents urged delay, being reluctant to send her into the hardships and partial solitude of the life that her fiancé would be obliged to take up for the next two years. The lovers therefore parted, John committing Rose to the care of his dearest friend, a man who was to him as Jonathan to David. "You will see," he said, "that Rose lacks no attention that you can give her. Be her escort and comrade and behave to her as a brother until I return." In all good faith the friend accepted the task. The result for John was a calamity. Without meaning to be disloyal, Rose and her lover's friend drifted into an intimacy which boded ill for John. He, poor fellow, eating his heart out in the loneliness of his distant encampment believed implicitly in Rose until, one day, letters came which undeceived him. Rose simply said, "I hope you will forgive me. I thought I loved you but I was mistaken. All my love belongs to Will, and the only shred of honor left to me is to tell you so. I send you back your ring and letters." What Will wrote I do not know.

Another story comes to me unfolded in a series of communications from a young woman who, feeling that she was needed at home and that she had not yet made preparation enough for a speedy marriage, sent her fiancé away from her side to accept a business position in a metropolitan city. The two had grown up together as girl and boy, had attended the same school, and been graduated from the same college. They had confessed their faith in Christ on the same day. If ever two persons appeared entirely suitable and congenial, they did. Yet the man meeting other and more polished girls in the city to which he went, girls who had known the benefit of social contact of which the little country maiden had no thought, found insensibly her image growing faded and indistinct. To do him justice he tried hard to maintain his position. Once and again he sent messages of almost agonized entreaty pleading with Ruth to name a day for their marriage. Months and years on one pretext or another she deferred this, until at last he wrote frankly asking a release from the engagement and explaining that he had found someone else who was willing to be his wife and whom he loved as he had never dreamed of loving before.

If there is any moral to be drawn from these illustrations, it is this: In a matter involving such consequences—an affair that reaches to the very roots of being—neither girls nor men should act with precipitation. Having plighted one's faith, suffer anything rather than prove unworthy.

It is perhaps too much to expect that people in love and about to marry shall think very much along the lines of so prosaic a subject as finance. At the altar the man will say, "With all my worldly goods I thee endow," which being interpreted should surely mean that a portion of his wealth or of his earnings should be hereafter at the bride's disposal. In the frequent conversations which an engaged couple carry on day after day during courtship, how seldom they touch on this practical theme. Yet if they are to marry, found a new family and carry on a home, it cannot be done without an income. The man owes it to his future lot to have something saved, something at least probably definite on which the two may live. Money will be required to maintain the very simplest household life. There are husbands who as bachelors formed a habit of close calculation and almost miserly economy in the effort to reach the competence they desired. They are not altogether to blame if it has never occurred to them that girls have not lived like the lilies of the field on air and sunshine.

It would be better for every reason if it were customary for these men as well as for their opposites who are spendthrifts by nature to sit down and count the cost, in actual dollars and cents, pencil and paper in hand, with the girl who is to share their common destiny. Reiterated protestations of love in time grow wearisome. A girl may not like to take the initiative and introduce this topic, and yet there may come for her when she is a wife a sad awakening if she finds that she has married a man who prefers to regard her as a privileged mendicant or a tolerated beggar rather than as an equal and a partner in business.

Let it not be forgotten that young people on the eve of marriage have been in training for maturity all their lives, and that habits have a tendency to crystallize into the concrete.

"Nowhere," says Dr. Henry Churchill King, "are the psychical and the physical so completely interwoven as in the phenomena of habit."

We come into this world freighted with tendencies which we have inherited, but these are less dominant than the habits which are formed for us in the beginning and which we form for ourselves as we go on. Habits of thought and of action make up our personality. For this if for no other reason, young people should remember that there may be antagonisms as well as attractions in the habits each may have formed.

In a recent romance of American life in which a marriage that started well turned out disastrously, the entering wedge of trouble manifested itself when the young husband flatly refused to give his wife money to buy postage stamps. He offered to procure anything she wanted if only she would state her wish. As she had been an independent wage earner it was extremely galling to be compelled to ask for every cent she needed.

A little candid conversation and planning, a frank mutual understanding on this one point, would save endless trouble after marriage.

The pastor of a church in New England one day thought it his duty to preach a sermon to his congregation on this very practical subject. A lady who was present was much amused at the haste with which a certain stingy deacon bundled his wife and daughters into their conveyance at the close of the service. "Heresy, heresy," he was heard to grumble. "Why can't the parson confine himself to spiritual matters?"

The habits of a lifetime had made the deacon unable to bear with patience the plain speech of his minister on a subject that had to do with the purse strings.

If a girl has been self-supporting and consequently independent, receiving a monthly or weekly salary and spending or saving it to suit herself, it is intensely uncomfortable for her to be treated as a child and given no freedom of choice in the management of money after marriage. Wherever it is practicable from the very beginning there should be a complete confidence on this matter, and it should not be left to confusion and haphazard, but should be arranged with fairness and discretion so that love may never be menaced by sordid considerations.

I am taking for granted that a girl assuming wifely duties and responsibilities does not intend to be reckless, irresponsible, and extravagant in this department of her life. Of this I shall speak in another chapter.

Chapter XII

Home-Keeping Hearts

STANDING on the threshold of womanhood and looking forth into the unknown future, a girl may see several paths and not know which to choose. Two theories obtain with those who have the responsibility of educating young women. One is based on the assumption that homemaking and domestic economy are no more distinctively feminine occupations than are buying and selling goods, entering a professional career, or engaging in any business beyond the home limits. The other, refusing to regard these outside callings as other than incidental, proceeds on the conviction that woman's most congenial sphere and her real kingdom are in the home. The latter theory is held by those who regard home as woman's principal field of service and most promising opportunity for happiness.

Personally, I go so far as to affirm my belief that only in home life does woman attain her best development and that whether married or single, home-keeping hearts are best.

In no circumstances that may be imagined can marriage be hallowed unless it is founded on reciprocal esteem and the purest love. Marriages of convenience, marriages for mercenary reasons, are simply invasions of the sacredness of a sacrament.

In the first flush of romantic youth, girls do not always understand the nature of lifelong obligations. They mistake sentiment for affection. Now and then a girl is full of a passionate desire to immolate herself on an altar of sacrifice. A man has a somewhat undesirable reputation. He is known to have wandered away from paths of rectitude, and forgathered with men of evil habits and wild courses. He may not have fallen so low as the prodigal in the parable, nor with the prodigal has he turned in humiliation and repentance from the darkness of sin, and sought again restoration in his father's house. A man who has done this, who has proved that repentance is real by an established reformation, may be worthy of the confidence of a girl whom he loves, and she may safely trust her life in his hands. Of such a man I am not writing. Such a man will be modest and slow to claim the honor of a pure woman's love until he has shown that he deserves it and that he has recovered the place he had lost.

A young enthusiastic girl is often attracted by a man who tells her in terms she only half comprehends that he has been drawn by bad companions into devious ways, but that if only she will trust him he will leave them and reform. Very seldom do promises of this sort made before marriage mean anything in the dreary future. In every community, in almost every street, there are instances of wretchedly shadowed homes wherein the man who was dissipated, intemperate, and immoral before marriage remains the same after marriage. His wife has not been strong enough to reform him. A girl should never take this risk for her own sake, for the sake of the man who asks so great a boon, and for the sake of her home.

I can think of fair lives laid waste in this fruitless effort, but never of one where the endeavor was crowned with success. In every such case parents, for the protection of their daughters, should insist on a sufficient period of probation before they give their consent to a marriage that may mean terrific shipwreck of the daughter's happiness and usefulness.

In order to insure true union in home life there should be no antagonism of creeds. People who accept opposite forms of faith would do well to hesitate long before they plight their troth. Entire accord in religion is a pledge of harmony. That will always be the happiest home of which it may be said that husband and wife are one in Christ, and that Christ is the Head of the house. Loving Him, they will not suffer estrangement and profanation to come upon their mutual love.

Nothing on earth is so divine as a home. It is four walls and a roof, with windows to let in the sunshine, and a door to bar against the outer world and to open to one's friends. It is a nest full of sweetness and peace. It is an asylum and a refuge and a shelter and a place of withdrawal from storm and tempest. It is a place of dignity and repose. In its best estate home is like heaven and home-keeping hearts are best.

Such a home need not be selfish. It may be like one that Dr. W. Robertson Nicoll has painted as the House of Perfect Hospitality. Of this house this veteran observer tells us that the guardian angel is the wife who is a perfect hostess, and who has the rare art of making everyone at ease who comes within the arc of her influence.

This is unfailingly true. You know how the spirit of the wife and mother penetrates the home, how she guides it, blesses it, and sets upon it the stamp of her personality. Some preparation for the office of homemaker should be included in the education of girls.

We are much too ready to fancy that this education must of necessity be domestic, and that if a girl knows how to cook and to sweep, to sew and to mend, if she has been trained in housekeeping she will be a successful homemaker. It does not follow, however, that the art of kneading bread and broiling steak is the art beyond others to make a girl happy in her marriage. She will discover before the honeymoon has waned that a devoted lover is not less devoted if he has a dinner that pleases him, and that a man is entitled to the prefix of saint if he bears without faultfinding a prolonged course of muddy coffee, soggy biscuits, and ruined meats; and yet no girl who has had the discipline of a good school or college need fear to undertake the direction of a home on this its lower plane. Recipe books with concise formulas and lucid explanations are not so abstruse as geometry and their cost is a trifle. A bright and clever woman may acquire everything she needs to know about housekeeping if she will give it her attention, in a very few weeks. A woman must be a miracle of stupidity if she cannot learn how to go to market, cook a dinner, and generally carry forward the work of an ordinary home, when this difficult task is accomplished without her brains and training by hundreds of raw recruits from the peasant homes of Ireland, Germany, Russia, Sweden, and Denmark, and by Orientals who have the additional handicap of belonging to an alien civilization. Believe me, girls, housekeeping is not a mysterious or occult science. Anybody who chooses can soon learn its secrets and order her home according to its precepts. She may have her mortifications and her difficult days, but these will pass and she will receive assistance from fellow housekeepers unless she is too proud to confess her ignorance.

If a young woman has been closely occupied in other directions she may be pardoned if she is not an adept in domestic science from the start. The probability is that nine out of ten of the girls whose eyes fall on these pages are already proficient in cooking, clear starching, fine laundry work, and similar pursuits since domestic science is taught in the public schools, in colleges, and working girls' clubs as a matter of course. Fortunate is the girl whose initiative has been taken under the watchful care of her mother in that mother's own kitchen.

What does one need to maintain herself in the center of her home and to make it the sweetest place to which a toiling man may turn, and the rallying point of every generous influence and every noble thought? She needs to be broadminded and hospitable to advancing ideas; she needs to be tactful and tender and above all things she requires common sense. This last attribute was conspicuously lacking in one of the most exquisite of George Eliot's characters, Dorothea Brooke, who committed the folly of marrying the Reverend Mr. Casaubon under the impression that she could best fulfill her mission in life by effacing herself and becoming a satellite of one who was simply a solemn humbug. Without the saving salt of common sense, a girl will fail to hold and keep her rightful position as the queen of a household.

John Ruskin, who had insight beyond that given to most men, in a famous passage has epitomized the story of the home.

> Now their separate characters are briefly these. The man's power is active, progressive, defensive. He is eminently the doer, the creator, the discoverer, the defender. His intellect is for speculation and invention; his energy for adventure, for war, and for conquest, whenever war is just, whenever conquest necessary. But the woman's power is for rule, not for battle; and her intellect is not for invention or creation, but for sweet ordering, arrangement and decision. She sees the qualities of things, their claims and their places. Her great function is praise; she enters into no conquest, but infallibly adjudges the crown of contest. By her office and place, she is protected from all danger and temptation. The man, in his rough work in the open world, must encounter all peril and trial,—to him therefore must be the failure, the offense, the inevitable error; often he must be wounded or subdued; often

misled; and *always* hardened. But he guards the woman from all this; within his house as ruled by her, unless she herself has sought it, need enter no danger, no temptation, no cause of error or offense. This is the true nature of home—it is the place of peace; the shelter, not only from all injury, but from all terror, doubt, and division. In so far as it is not this, it is not home; so far as the anxieties of the outer life penetrate into it, and the inconsistently minded, unknown, unloved, or hostile society of the outer world is allowed by either husband or wife to cross the threshold, it ceases to be home; it is then only a part of that outer world which you have roofed over and lighted fire in. But so far as it is a sacred place, a vestal temple, a temple of the hearth watched over by household gods, before whose faces none may come but those whom they can receive with love,—so far as it is this, and roof and fire are types only of a nobler shade and light, shade of the rock in a weary land, and light as of the Pharos in the stormy sea,—so far it vindicates the name and fulfills the praise of home.

And wherever a true wife comes, this home is always round her. The stars only may be over her head, the glowworm in the night-cold grass may be the only fire at her foot, but home is yet wherever she is; and for a noble woman it stretches far round her, better than ceiled with cedar or painted with vermilion, shedding its quiet light far, for those who else were homeless.

In this day a girl though unmarried may have her own home. If she has wealth it may be an ample house with a retinue of servants, while if she is a wage earner or a woman of small but fixed income, it may be a tiny apartment or a bit of a cottage where she may live alone or with a single maid. Several girls may combine and on a cooperative plan furnish rooms and maintain a delightful home. Girl-colonies are by no means rare in our cities and a half-dozen students, journalists, artists, or businesswomen living together with an elder sister or a mother to chaperon them and look after the details of housewifery, are much more comfortably situated than they can possibly be in boarding and they have also the privacy and dignity of a true home. Among the most beautiful of homes are those in which live women consecrated to Christian service and wearing the uniform of the deaconness. Their homes are eminently attractive and though their lives are crowded with tasks and their visiting the sick and the poor and ministering to the aged leaves them little space for recreation and little leisure, still they have hours of relaxation when they, too, know the blessedness of being under their own roof. They can testify in their self-denying lives that home-keeping hearts are best.

The externals, furniture and appointments of the home, have little to do with its comfort and its joy. The hearth-fire burns as brightly for the poor as for the rich. If covetousness, envy, jealousy, and misunderstanding are warded from the home and contentment, sincerity, confidence, and tranquillity reign there it will reach home's highest ideal.

There's but the meager crust, Love,
There's but the measured cup;
On scanty fare we breakfast,
On scanty fare we sup.
Yet be not thou discouraged,
Nor falter on the way,
Since Wealth is for a life, Love,
And Want is for a day.

Our robes are hodden gray, Love.
Ah! would that thine were white,
And shot with gleams of silver,
And rich with golden light.
Yet care not thou for raiment,
But climb, as pilgrims may,
Since Ease is for a life, Love,
And Toil is for a day.

Our shelter oft is rude, Love;
We feel the chilling dew,
And shiver in the darkness

Which silent stars shine through.
Yet shall we seek our palace,
And there in gladness stay,
Since Home is for a life, Love,
And Travel for a day.

The heart may sometimes ache, Love,
The eyes grow dim with tears;
Slow glide the hours of sorrow,
Slow beats the pulse of fears.
Yet patience with the evil,
For, though the good delay,
Still Joy is for a life, Love,
And Pain is for a day.

Chapter XIII

Heroines

WHEN WE speak of a heroine, there arises before us a picture of someone who in sore straits has shown dauntless courage and braved with fortitude the uttermost pains of life and the pangs of death. Margaret Wilson standing in the water as the tide came in, refusing while it mounted higher and higher until it reached her lips to deny her Lord, is a heroine that all Scotland reveres.

Catherine Douglas thrusting her bare arm as a bolt into the door that she might keep a fiendish mob from entering the room, beneath which she knew the king was hidden, was a heroine.

So, too, was the tenderly nurtured wife of Dr. Judson in those dark days in India when her husband lay in prison and she went from door to door fearless and resolute, although she had to beg the Hindu mothers to nurse the famishing babe she held in her arms. The annals of the martyrs are starred with the names of those who failed not nor faltered in the hour of agony. Even so lately as in the autumn of 1905 at Lienchow, China, Dr. Eleanor Chestnut, facing her murderers calmly, pleaded for the lives of the young missionaries who had only that day reached the field where they were to die. Dr. Chestnut, Mrs. Machle, little

Amy, Mrs. Peele; five years earlier Miss Morrill and Miss Gould were heroines of the rarest type. Earth never lacks them for the noble army of martyrs never vanishes from the world.

The heroines I am thinking of today have no grand opportunities to show their splendid qualities, as have had martyrs and confessors since the dawn of the Christian era. I have not the slightest doubt that there are heroines reading this book; heroines who would blush did they hear the name applied to their modest selves. Among the girls who are toiling uncomplainingly for others, with never a single selfish plan or motive, there are any number who jostle us on the street, who stand behind counters, who are binding shoes and stitching gloves and sitting at the typewriter and footing up long columns of figures that they may relieve aged parents or assist in bringing up little brothers and sisters. The maid who works in the kitchen, her people far across the ocean in Norway or Sweden or Denmark or in green Erin or the German's Fatherland, is often enough a heroine. She is a young girl not much beyond twenty or twenty-five, though the drudgery of her days has made her look older. She is up in the morning long before you are, my sweet Dorothy, building a fire, sweeping a room, cooking a breakfast, doing her best to make the house a comfortable place for you and the rest of the family. I have told a story before somewhere else, but I venture to tell it again: the story of woman whose humble but useful office it was to cook for a New York boardinghouse.

She had lived in that house eleven faithful years, and very few of the people above stairs had ever seen her. One summer Sunday morning an urgent message from the kitchen was sent to the mistress, who hurried down to find the cook gasping for breath. "Oh, Miss Agnes," she exclaimed, "I think I'm dying. Who'll get the breakfast?"

That question was her last conscious utterance. In a

moment she had passed beyond these clamorous voices and these daily needs. But if ever a heroine lived she lived in the person of this obscure, diligent, efficient daily toiler.

Some of us have no right to let unselfish people put on the halo of the heroine because of our heedlessness: "But evil is wrought by want of thought as well as want of heart." When the pretty daughter of the house wears so many elaborate dresses that the laundry maid, no older than herself, drags a weary frame to bed; when the indolence of one person is indulged at the expense of another, the first must answer in the day of account for the sin of having made somebody a heroine. All toilers are not heroines nor is work, however arduous, anything but a blessing. The busy bees do not have to kill time, and killing time is the hardest work and the least profitable on the planet. Heroines are never self-conscious. If you fancy yourself to have earned a place on their honor roll, you are probably the only one who would dream of writing your name there.

I think of a sweet-faced girl who went year by year, day in and day out, to an office where her duties were many and the calls upon her unremitting. She never took a vacation. When it was suggested in hot summer weeks that she could be spared, she calmly put the idea aside, and when finally she grew pale and wan and at last was ill and obliged to go to a hospital, it was ascertained that her entire life had been an offering at the shrine of a father who, though strong and able-bodied, chose to consider himself an invalid. Gladys at last came no more to the office. Her life work was done. She had been a heroine to the last.

So it was with one of the bravest women I ever knew, a woman who in her early girlhood exchanged wealth for poverty in a single day. Undauntedly, she grasped the nettle of adverse fortune and started out to see what she might find to do. The thing she found was the writing about fashions for a weekly periodical. She said, "I will write about fashions as an artist paints or a gardener plants or a poet dreams. To this humble field of literary work I will devote the best of my powers." For more than twenty years, through storm and sun, through summer's heat and winter's cold, toward the last through pain and weariness due to a lingering disease this brave woman did her work. She was a young girl when it began, she was middle-aged when it closed, and through all she was a heroine.

There is a touching little poem of which I do not know the authorship, but it has a very true note and I am sure when you read it you will feel with me that it tells a story of heroism.

In the one poor room that was all their home,
A mother lay on the bed,
Her seven young children around her;
And, calling the eldest, she said:

"I'm going to leave you, Mary;
You're nearly fourteen, you know;
And now you must be a good girl, dear,
And make me easy to go.

"You can't depend much on father;
But just be patient, my child,
And keep the children out of his way
Whenever he comes home wild.

"And keep the home as well you can;
And, little daughter, think
He didn't used to be so;
Remember, it's all the drink."

The weeping daughter promised
Always to do her best;
And, closing her eyes on a weary life,
The mother entered her rest.

And Mary kept her promise,
As faithfully as she might;

She cooked and washed and mended,
And kept things tidy and bright.

And the little chubby fingers lost
Their childish softness and grace,
And roughened and chapped and calloused;
And the rosy, childish face,

Grew thin, and haggard, and anxious,
Careworn, tired, and old,
As on those slender shoulders
The burdens of life were rolled.

So, when the heated season
Burned pitiless overhead,
And up from the filth of the noisome street
The fatal fever spread,

The work and want and drunken blows
Had weakened the tender frame,
And into the squalid room once more
The restful shadow came.

And Mary sent for the playmate
Who lived just over the way,
And said, "The charity doctor
Has been here, Katie, today.

"He says I'll never be better,
The fever has been so bad;
And if it wasn't for one thing,
I'm sure I'd just be glad.

"It isn't about the children;
I've kept my promise good,
And mother will know I stayed with them
As long as ever I could.

"But you know how it's been here, Katie—
I've had so much to do,
I couldn't mind the children
And go to the preaching too.

"And I've been so tired-like at night,
I couldn't think to pray;
And now, when I see the Lord Jesus,
What ever am I to say?"

And Katie, the little comforter,
Her help to the problem brought;
And into that heart made wise by love,
The Spirit sent this thought:

"I wouldn't say a word, dear,
For sure He understands;
I wouldn't say ever a word at all,
But, Mary, just show Him your hands!"

It's a comfort, is it not, that up in heaven there is a Friend who sees and comprehends the self-denials and sacrifices of those who love Him. No alabaster box is ever broken in vain. No little service ever passes unnoticed by the One who sees the falling of the sparrow, although sparrows are so common and cheap that two of them are sold for a farthing.

I would not have you think that heroines always die in their youth. That used to be the fault of many good books, the lives of the saints too often led to an early grave. Heroines live to a good old age, just as those do who never have been heroic but merely dull, self-seeking, and vain.

One of my heroines had the great misfortune when a very young girl to stumble over a rough place in the road. That trifling fall laid her aside for years and years. She could no longer go abroad or walk a step, but her sunny room and her window were magnets that drew to her everyone in the village. She made her pain a daily offering to Christ and said nothing about it. There are girls who cheerfully deny themselves luxuries and go without comforts that they may give largely to the cause of missions or to some favorite charity. The pastor of a city church was one day passing through his Sunday school when a teacher gently asked him to stop. She slipped into his hand a large roll of bills. "My sister and I were not at church this morning," she said, "but I have brought our offering."

The sisters were teachers in a primary school and their home was a tenement in a very plain quarter of the town. When the minister saw that their gift was a hundred dollars, he hesitated a little.

"Miss Amy," he said, "ought you and Miss Jessie to give so much?"

He did not add that very few of the rich in the congregation approximated this amount in their annual contribution.

"Oh," said Amy, a smile flashing over her face and making it lovely, "every dollar there is a joy to sister and me."

There are women who have cheerfully worked from early youth to the end almost of a long life that they may have the great pleasure of giving to the Lord they love, and helping to bring His kingdom of grace to the world.

Sometimes we may show heroism, we girls, by living cheerfully and patiently in homes that are uncongenial. People outside do not dream it, but our own folk are not always easy to get on with. They are captious, irritable, and faultfinding. It may even be that for some reason a father or mother may have trying ways. We may have to bear disappointments. If we do so bravely, if we are amiable when others are capricious, if we receive everything as coming straight from God's hand, we may be heroines.

Meek souls there are who little dream
Their daily life an angel's theme;
Or that the rod they bear so calm
In heaven may be a martyr's palm.

I wouldn't be cross, dear, it's never worth while;
Disarm the vexation by wearing a smile;
Let hap a disaster, a trouble, a loss,
Just meet the thing boldly, and never be cross.
No bitterness sweetens, no sharpness may heal

The wound which the soul is too proud to reveal.
No envy hath peace; by a fret and a jar
The beautiful work of our hands we may mar.
Let happen what may, dear, of trouble and loss,
I wouldn't be cross, love, I wouldn't be cross.

Chapter XIV

A Little Nonsense

I HARDLY know what you will think of the advice I am about to give. But I often feel that a girl may be quite too serious, may take too gloomy a view of things in general, and may spend time in reflection that might much better be devoted to pure fun. Never be afraid of a little frivolity at the right time and in the right place. It is just as necessary to have pleasure as we go along as to do our work, and most of us work better for a little play. A girl without a sense of humor is sadly handicapped her life long. There are many situations which would be wholly unbearable if we could not get a little amusement out of them. Some part of every day should be illuminated by mirth and gladness. Girls are sometimes reproved by solemn elders, who have lived past the age of bubbling merriment, because they laugh too much. Why should they not laugh at the drolleries that they see and hear, and why should older people be censorious when young girls giggle? Giggling may not be dignified, but dignity is not the only thing worth having in this world. When the lambs frisk in the spring, when children romp and shout, they are simply tossing off the effervescence of gay spirits appropriate to their age. Exuberant vitality belongs to youth and not only is there no harm in it but it is positively right and therefore charming. A disposition that frowns upon nonsense and is offended at gaiety acts as a wet blanket on the enjoyment of others. I am not pleading for affectation or insincerity or for an insensibility to the real needs and aims of life. But the day's work is as well done by those who enjoy an innocent jest, a good story, and a bright anecdote as by their companions who are dull and heavy and have no sparkle or gleam to enliven the task. Very good people are sometimes hopelessly tedious and become bores to their friends because they never see anything but the literal and prosaic side of conduct.

A good example of what I mean is found in the characters Lady Catherine de Bourgh and Mr. Collins, the lumpish clergyman, who though as good as gold in some respects was a dead weight in society because of his colossal self-conceit and lack of wit and humor. Miss Austen was the daughter of a clergyman and had no doubt suffered more or less from the denseness of curates in charge, from whom she drew her masterpiece in the person of Mr. Collins.

Girls of course remember that loveliest of young women, Elizabeth Bennet, who is the heroine of *Pride and Prejudice.* Some of her encounters with Lady Catherine and that gentlewoman's satellite, Mr. Collins, are as entertaining to us as they must have been to the people who were living when Miss Austen wrote. For instance, Lady Catherine addressing the peerless Elizabeth asks,

> "Do you play and sing, Miss Bennet?"
>
> "A little."
>
> "Oh! then—some time or other we shall be happy to hear you. Our instrument is a capital one, probably superior to—You shall try it some day. Do your sisters play and sing?"
>
> "One of them does."
>
> "Why did not you all learn? You ought all to have learned. The Miss Webbs all play, and their father has not so good an income as yours. Do you draw?"

"No, not at all."

"What, none of you?"

"Not one."

"That is very strange. But I suppose you had no opportunity. Your mother should have taken you to town every spring for the benefit of masters."

"My mother would have had no objection, but my father hates London."

"Has your governess left you?"

"We never had any governess."

"No governess! I never heard of such a thing. Your mother must have been quite a slave to your education."

Elizabeth could hardly help smiling as she assured her that had not been the case.

"Then, who taught you? Who attended to you? Without a governess, you must have been neglected."

"Compared with some families, I believe we were; but such of us as wished to learn never wanted the means. We were always encouraged to read, and had all the masters that were necessary. Those who chose to be idle, certainly might."

"Aye, no doubt; but that is what a governess will prevent, and if I had known your mother, I should have advised her most strenuously to engage one. I always say that nothing is to be done in education without steady and regular instruction, and nobody but a governess can give it. It is wonderful how many families I have been the means of supplying in that way. I am always glad to get a young person well placed out. Four nieces of Mrs. Jenkinson are most delightfully situated through my means; and it was but the other day that I recommended another young person, who was merely accidentally mentioned to me, and the family are quite delighted with her. Mrs. Collins," addressing the clergyman's wife, "did I tell you of Lady Metcalfe's calling yesterday to thank me? She finds Miss Pope a treasure. 'Lady Catherine,' said she, 'you have given me a treasure.' Are any of your younger sisters out, Miss Bennet?"

"Yes, ma'am, all."

"All! What, all five out at once? Very odd! And you only the second. The younger ones out before the elder are married! Your younger sisters must be very young?"

"Yes, my youngest is not sixteen. Perhaps *she* is full young to be much in company. But really, ma'am, I think it would be very hard upon younger sisters, that they should not have their share of society and amusement, because the elder may not have the means or inclination to marry early. The last-born has as good a right to the pleasures of youth as the first. And to be kept back on *such* a motive! I think it would not be very likely to promote sisterly affection or delicacy of mind."

"Upon my word," said her ladyship, "you give your opinion very decidedly for so young a person. Pray, what is your age?"

"With three sisters grown up," replied Elizabeth, "your ladyship can hardly expect me to own it."

Lady Catherine seemed quite astonished at not receiving a direct answer; and Elizabeth suspected herself to be the first creature who had ever dared to trifle with so much dignified impertinence.

"You cannot be more than twenty, I am sure,—therefore you need not conceal your age."

"I am not one and twenty."

For a person not yet twenty-one Elizabeth Bennet held her own very well when pitted against so formidable an antagonist as Lady Catherine. She had already in a much more delicate encounter allowed Mr. Collins to see that he had no chance of success as a suitor for her hand. Whereupon he speedily consoled himself elsewhere. The little scene throws a spotlight on several phases of girlhood's estate as it used to be. The education of English girls of good family in the eighteenth century was almost wholly conducted at home and was frequently very limited in comparison with that accorded to twentieth-century girls. Our girls presumably have better times. At all events they have the environment which makes for more variety and less monotony than was the portion of their youthful great-grandmothers. It is of little importance, however, what the environment is or what the period, if only the girl herself has in her the stuff for both work and play and knows how to use tools that are put in her hands.

An eminent writer has said, "Never chew your pills." People who have no sense of fun are always chewing their pills instead of swallowing them, and tasting only the sugar-coat. Let us see what Dr. W. Robertson Nicoll has to say about this. There is a little sermon in it for some girl who takes life by the hardest end, and seldom gets the good she might because she is always afraid that she will somehow blunder or somehow hurt another by setting a bad example. If I could I would broadcast over the land this bit of counsel,

> Don't stop to think too much about the example you set, or the impression you are making. Simply be good; be trustful. Be sincere. Be yourself. And let impression and example take care of themselves.
>
> Never chew your pills, that is, the best way to deal with anything disagreeable is to have it ended as soon as may be, and then leave it. The chewing of imaginary pills is the worst error of all, and goes further to weaken and impoverish life than almost any other habit. In Saint Theresa's *Book of the Foundations*, she tells us how she went to find her convent at Salamanca. The first night was spent in a half-ruined house out of which some students had been turned. The nun who was with the saint was very nervous, and said in the night, "I am thinking, mother, if I should die here what you would do alone." It was the night before All Souls and all the bells of the university city were ringing. This sound increased the fear of the nun, but Saint Theresa boldly answered, "When this event happens, sister, I will think what I ought to do. For the present, let me sleep."

Nonsense has its legitimate place in life, but we must not confuse nonsense with buffoonery or folly or the levity that never appreciates the occasion for earnestness. When the wise man compared the laughter of fools to the crackling of thorns under a pot, he probably had in mind those brainless beings who indulge in ill-timed jests, make fun of sacred things, and take pleasure in disturbing the comfort of quiet listeners who are not in a mood for pleasantry. Kindness is the truest wisdom of life and we cannot go far without it. Fun should never be indulged at the expense of the feelings of a friend, and laughter in which there is a covert sneer is malicious and hateful.

If you really cannot understand or appreciate nonsense verses, do not pretend that you like them. I have seen people gravely unresponsive to the fun of a limerick or shocked at its absurdity, but I liked them better for their sincerity than if they had made a pretense of amusement which was not real. Fun is the birthright of some fortunate souls. Others not having the natural endowment have to fare along as best they can without its bright accompaniment on their way.

If you do not appreciate it yourself, there is the greater reason that you should not condemn it in others. Beware of clouding the horizon for your neighbors because you prefer gray to rose-color.

There is less danger of this than there used to be. A sweet girl of sixteen, years ago in childlike trust, put her hand in that of her Savior and stood with a circle of young people in front of the congregation confessing her love and loyalty to Christ. A few days later she was the center of a merry group and her laugh rang out like a silver bell as someone told a story that pleased her. She had always been the life of any company in which she took part. Her great-aunt, sitting by a window overlooking the garden, shook her gray head sorrowfully and turning to a friend remarked, "I was afraid of this. It is what I predicted. I begged Emily's mother not to consent to her joining the church. There she is, full of fun and laughing just as she always has, apparently not a serious thought in her head." The ideal of the old gentlewoman was distorted. There was no reason in the world why a child of Christ who was following Him should cease to be happy and gay, while there was every reason that she should continue to be cheerful and merry-hearted as she had hitherto been.

In my own girlhood I was a visitor one summer at a manse in the country, and as I stayed some weeks and often drove about with the old pastor as he went over hill and dale to call on parishioners, I came to know quite well the stories of people who lived on outlying farms, miles from the village.

One day the old black mare stopped of her own accord at a tumbledown gate. A straggling path bordered with holly-hocks in bloom led up to a weatherbeaten porch. An old lady, crippled with rheumatism, sat there in an armchair. A dispirited-looking man, dejection in every line of his face and in the droop of his patient shoulders, came out to greet the preacher.

"Jenny won't pass your house, friend," said the minister, "and I am going to have a chat with your mother. I hope things are going well."

"Things are worse than ever," was the melancholy reply. But immediately a smile flickered like a sunbeam across the weary face. "Hattie's coming home tomorrow," said the man.

After we were on the road again, the good pastor explained that Hattie, the eldest daughter of the house, who was a teacher in a distant city and the main support of an impoverished house, was expected to spend her vacation, "and," he added, "I want you to see her. Hattie is the strongest, sweetest, and most lovable girl in the world and no matter how thick the troubles may be, she never loses hope and courage. She is always overflowing with fun."

Sometimes I think that a girl can have no better mission in life than to cheer a despondent father and help a burdened mother, and once in a while it is borne in upon me that the gift girlhood has of simple mirth, even of immoderate laughter at trifles, and of the giggles that try the cynic's patience are not gifts to despise. They do their part in making this old world a good place to live in.

Chapter XV

To Please People

JOHN RUSKIN in one of his delightful essays has told girls that part of their duty in life is to please people. Wordsworth in a famous stanza crystallizes his thought of the sex as,

> *A perfect woman nobly planned,*
> *To warn, to comfort and command;*
> *A creature not too bright or good*
> *For human nature's daily food.*

In other words a being whose office in life was to make those around her happy. What qualities do we need in order to be pleasing? No doubt the very first is freedom from self-consciousness, and the next an instinctive altruism that makes us ready and willing to put our own concerns aside that we may devote time and thought to those of the home-people, of our friends, and our associates in business and society.

Self-consciousness is a hampering condition from which it is very difficult to escape. It may not ruin good manners but it injures their effect, cramps personality, and gives good people an unfortunate manner. Intense absorption in self produces the egotist, and an egotist invariably sees life as it colors his individual hopes and wishes. One who is most occupied with the first person singular is handicapped fatally in the race, and will never succeed very well in pleasing his neighbor.

One of the lessons we need to learn is that of living agreeably with others and working in easy adjustment with them. You may be clever to your fingertips, a genius, an artist, or a poet. You may be honorable in your dealings and generous in your intentions and still you may be brusque, rude, and discourteous so that your good qualities are blurred and marred, and your character presents a distorted image to the world. If we are continually insisting on having our own way, if we are reluctant to yield a little to the wishes of our friends, we shall antagonize rather than please in the contacts of the day.

A mother was one day talking about her daughters, who were girls of unusual distinction and charm. In her family the daughters had come before the sons, and there were several active little fellows, boisterous and rollicking as boys are apt to be, and these were sometimes left in the care of the elder sisters. The mother was going away for a little while, and it was her custom when absent to delegate authority and leave the younger children in the care of one sister and the housekeeping in the care of the other. In these departments the girls took turns. "When it is Marion's turn to look after the boys, I am never quite at rest," said the mother. "I have an undertone of uneasiness to carry because I am sure there will be friction. Marion is judicious but she is arbitrary. Her rule is absolute. She issues commands, and if the boys do not obey her she very likely sends them to bed. I hear complaints on my return and I find poor Marion something of a wreck. Elizabeth, on the contrary, conciliates. She has a wonderful gift of tact. She gets into the heart of the boys, understands how they feel, makes allowances for their energy, and manages to have a beautiful time with them. Of my two daughters, I suppose

Marion is the stronger and it may be the finer in some ways, but Elizabeth is far the easier to live with."

Once when visiting a New England college I met a girl who was not beautiful nor especially studious, who at first did not impress me as remarkable, but whom I presently discovered to be the most popular member of her class. Everyone consulted her. She seemed to be a leader in what I may call college politics. During the busy weeks that precede commencement, when affairs crowd one another in the college world, this girl appeared able to reconcile differences, settle disputes, and generally arrange the order of events. "What is her secret?" I asked a veteran professor.

"Dorothy's secret?" said the lady. "Why it is partly personal magnetism, partly training, partly an innate and winsome sweetness. Have you noticed that her manners are perfect? She is never in a hurry, she is deferential to those older than herself, she is lovely to her juniors, she is polite with the politeness that is born in some people and that others acquire only by strife and toil."

I hold that good manners are within the reach of us all. Temperaments differ. Some of us are impetuous, some of us are deliberate. This makes no real difference in results if we restrain ourselves at need, and cultivate the arts of consideration and gentleness in human intercourse. A well-bred person is rude to no one. For instance, there may be two girls of the same age who meet incidentally in the commonplace business of buying and selling ribbon. The girl behind the ribbon counter and the girl in front of it are equally on a plane when the matter is one of good manners. Each is in a position to exercise a little patience and a little courtesy, and the one is no whit superior to the other nor is there any room for patronage and condescension in the buyer or for curtness and incivility in the seller. Matching ribbons takes time and sometimes invades patience, as when one young woman is obliged to wait upon a half-dozen eager customers almost at once.

A young girl who came to New York a stranger and found work in a department store, was advanced from post to post so rapidly that her success elicited comment. The business manager explained it in a sentence: "Miss Elverson is extremely exact and she has an amazing talent for selling goods; she has charming manners."

Another young woman about the same time came to the metropolis from a distant southern city, came without acquaintances or introductions and with a very slender sum of money in her purse. She was looking for work on a newspaper, and she presently found something to do. In the course of twelve months she rose from obscurity to a place of conspicuous service, and before the end of the second year she was socially sought in homes of refinement and exclusiveness, an invitation to which was in itself a compliment. How did it happen? There was no accident about it, for this girl had talent, perseverance, womanly grace, and manners that won her immediate recognition wherever she went.

Granted ability and faithfulness, with the addition of an agreeable manner, obstacles will vanish from the path.

If we would succeed in pleasing people we must take a genuine interest. You cannot go through the world holding your head high and looking with disdain on those who do not particularly appeal to you and at the same time give pleasure as you go.

To plume one's self on birth or family standing, education, or any advantage that has been bestowed upon one is weak and foolish: "What hast thou that thou didst not receive?"

The judgment of those whose opinions are not always sought is apt to go straight to the mark. If the washerwoman and the day laborer and the brakeman and the deckhand speak well of you, your manners are probably good. Some years ago I knew a man so knightly, so courtly, so beautiful in all his life that to know him was a joy. His manner was as courteous to an old woman carrying home a basket of kindling wood picked up beside a building, as to the most distinguished lady in the circle of his friends. He would rise as quickly to give a seat in a crowded streetcar to the woman with a shawl over her head, as to her neighbor dressed in velvet and furs. This man belonged to the editorial staff of a morning newspaper, and it was his habit in the gray dawn to take a ferry on his homeward way. One summer he dropped his work and went across the Atlantic for a few weeks' vacation. To a deckhand on the ferryboat he said, "I am going on a holiday for some weeks, and you will not see me again until I return from England."

The weatherbeaten face lit up. "Are you going to London?" said the man.

"Yes," was the reply. "What can I do for you there?"

"If you wouldn't mind going to see my old mother and telling her that you know her boy, I would be the happiest fellow on earth."

"Tell me where she lives," said my friend, taking a card from his pocket and writing the address of the deckhand's mother. "You may depend on my going."

To make the little visit, which involved a short railway journey and some special planning, took a day out of the week allotted to London, but my friend who loved to please people willingly gave the day; and when he came home he grasped the hand of his English friend and told him how they were faring in the little cottage among the roses, told him of the cup of tea that he drank with the mother, and gave the loving messages she sent to her lad over the leagues of ocean.

This was a little thing perhaps, but it was one of the little things that nobody would have thought of unless he liked to give people pleasure. Since that summer my friend has crossed another sea, and is doing God's errands in another part of God's great universe. I often like to think that he still does errands of kindness in his heavenly home.

Conventional rules are a great convenience. It is well to know how to do things, to be at ease in society, to feel no awkwardness, and to be free from any thought about the impression one is making. Better than any book of etiquette to this end is a kind heart. Good manners are the outward expression of inward grace. Those who possess them make it their mission to scatter sunshine on shadowed paths. They never stoop to anything mean or low. They would not for the world speak unkindly of the absent. They take pains to entertain a tedious visitor, to speak so plainly that the deaf can hear them, to set bashful people and strangers at ease, and to amuse diffident boys who are at the trying age when they are passed over because they are too young or too old for the company in which they find themselves.

Some of us are very anxious about visiting cards and forms and ceremonies, and fear lest we shall in some minor matter violate the code of good society. Let me tell you, girls, that you may as well give yourselves no disturbance on trivial subjects of this kind. The manners of good society are everywhere the same. The etiquette of the visiting card is very easily acquired. The gracious art of pleasing is as useful and as often illustrated in a lonely cabin on the mountain-side as in the most sumptuous residence in the land. Good manners have been trampled upon before now in high places. The art of pleasing people is not mastered by everyone.

I would suggest that we make a sacrifice day by day of our own wishes, our discontent, perhaps our vanity, and study to be courteous to everyone for Christ's sake. There are those whom we meet on the daily path whose faces glow as from an inner light. They reflect the beauty of spirit which reigns in our Elder Brother. His likeness is stamped on their faces. They more than others understand how to please people as the Bible says, "for their good to edification."

My neighbor met me on the street,
She dropped a word of greeting gay,
Her look so bright, her tone so sweet,
I stepped to music all that day.

The cares that tugged at heart and brain,
The work too heavy for my hand,
The ceaseless underbeat of pain,
The tasks I could not understand,

Grew brighter as I walked along,
With air and step of liberty,
Freed by the sudden lilt of song
That filled the world with cheer for me.

Yet was this all. A woman wise,
Her life enriched by many a year,
Had faced me with her grave, true eyes,
Passed on, and said, "Good morning, dear!"

Chapter XVI

Right and Wrong in Recreation

LOOKING over my mail one morning, I found a letter in a girlish hand unknown to me. There is a curious sort of freemasonry about letters; something mysterious and vital that makes them different from anything else on the globe. Before I open a letter, whether from friend or stranger, I often forecast its contents and make a rather correct guess as to its probable message for me. I take an interest in postmarks and, if somebody writes me from Manitoba or Afghanistan or Kalamazoo or Bombay, I am aware before I cut the envelope that a waft of reality from village or bungalow or castle or business office is coming straight into my little den. Letters often reach me from girls of whom I never heard until I read their names at the bottom of the last page, but once we have been introduced in that simple fashion, these girls are my friends. Maybe it was from Seattle, maybe from Mobile, maybe from Pensacola—it does not matter where—that a girl poured out her heart on the question of amusements. Would it be right for her to do this, or wrong for her to do that? Could she without violating her conscience and staining the white surface of her mind with sin read such a novel, or go to hear and see such an opera, or accept an invitation to a house where she knew there would be a dance and where the people were good, but worldly? She emphasized the last words; evidently she wanted me to know that her friends were reputable people, honored in the community, and she also wished to convey the idea that they were not religious in a sense which she had been taught to attach to the term, "Good but worldly." I pondered over it a while before I dared to answer my little friend.

Jesus said in that last wonderful prayer of His for His disciples, "I pray not that Thou shouldst take them out of the world, but that Thou shouldst keep them from the evil." Every night and morning when we kneel beside our beds we pray, "Lead us not into temptation, but deliver us from evil." Our greatest desire should be, if we are true Christians, to be kept unspotted from the world. But God has put us in the world not to look down upon it nor to shun it nor draw our garments away from it, but to live in, labor in, and love it. The people around us are people of the world as we are; of this world, not of another. One of the coming days a door will open for you and me into a world we have not seen, but while we are here it is our privilege to make the world our sphere of action and of influence. We do not believe in shutting ourselves up in cells or in retiring from the social scene. We do believe that we ought to carry the spirit of piety and consecration wherever we go.

Some of our objections to forms of amusement common in the world and entirely refined and unobjectionable are based purely on tradition. At one time there were very few novels fit for the reading of a delicate-minded and innocent young girl. The novels familiar to the student of our earlier English literature are defaced by coarseness and vulgarity that are not tolerated now. They are not redeemed by features of compelling interest, and one wonders that they were ever admitted into the libraries of fastidious people; even great genius does not condone shocking immodesty.

Doubtless the objection formerly made most sweepingly against all novels in the hands of young people had its root in the fact that much that was written by men of genius, when imaginative literature first came over from Italy to England, was unfit for women's reading.

The best literature we have today, the flower of culture and the perfection of insight, is found in the literary form of the novel. It would be idle to forbid girls the reading of novels. To bar this door from them would be to exclude them from a realm of pleasure and to abridge their opportunity of learning from life, as it is revealed in letters.

Formerly, too, the stage was universally gross and profane. It was taken for granted that actors and actresses were people necessarily of low tastes and immoral lives. The theater therefore was justly condemned as a place to be avoided by those who led clean lives, who hated unseemly jests, and who feared God and kept His commandments. I do not presume in this chapter to defend the novel, the theater, the opera, or any form or place of recreation that was once condemned but may now have thrown off glaring defects that at one time were odious. I simply wish to lay down this rule as one which has no exception; if you cannot go to see a play of Shakespeare presented on the stage without an uncomfortable qualm of conscience, stay away. If you look upon novel reading merely as a waste of time, read history and essays and leave novels on the library shelves. Apply the rule everywhere and establish it as a principle that you will not trifle with conscientious scruples.

On the other hand, avoid being narrow. Do not condemn others for doing under proper restraints and in proper conditions what they think to be right, even though to you it may seem wrong. The whole question of amusement is very easily settled if only one bring everything to the test, Would I be willing to do this, to go there, or to engage in the other if I knew this were my last day on earth or if I felt conscious that my Savior were in the company? We never do go if we are Christians anywhere that our Savior is not with us, and for any one of us the morning that has dawned may possibly be the last we shall spend here on earth.

When our Savior was here He was a man of His time. We do not find that He was an ascetic. He did not neglect society. He went to feasts and to weddings, and we may be sure that His smile in those gatherings was like the rising of the sun.

Perhaps the best way for my correspondent and others like her to decide the vexing question of amusements, their right or their wrong, is to ask, What is the best use to which I can put my hours of recreation? Please do not forget that recreation and rest are right, that there is no special virtue in holding one's self from all of pleasant society. When we go to a social entertainment of any kind we are bound to carry to it some contribution. We must give as well as get. A girl should take pains to cultivate the social side of her nature as well as the intellectual and spiritual. A college president said to me not long ago, speaking of his beautiful eighteen-year-old daughter, "I want her to be developed as an all-round woman, and yet to keep the heart of a child."

The heart of a child! Is not this the best that can happen to any of us, to lose none of the freshness and zest of childhood, to be easily pleased, to expect something new and bright just around the corner, and to find delight in little things? One cannot but be sorry for a young girl who is blasé, who cares only for costly entertainments, and for whom simplicity has no charm.

Part of a girl's mission in life should be to entertain her family and friends. There are long winter evenings when a common bond should unite the household and draw it more closely together. Perhaps there is a grandmother whose eyes are growing dim, or whose hearing is less acute than once, and for her the evenings are somewhat wearisome. There may be a young brother who listens for a whistle from a comrade out-of-doors, and slips off to spend an hour or two in company of which his parents would not approve could they know the effect it was having on the lad's character. Father and mother are often too tired to read at the end of the day, but they enjoy a game in which old and young may have a share. It is a girl's province to suggest agreeable ways of spending home evenings and to take the lead in home entertainment. Here there can be no question of right or wrong; the obligation being plain. Very likely some self-denial is involved in giving up one's personal inclination, and doing what merely passes time for the rest. But very few girls dislike self-denial. It is one of those virtues which sweeten existence for us, making us understand that giving is better than receiving.

I would have every girl add to her more practical knowledge some skill in playing chess or checkers, some deftness in the ordinary and amusing games which, from time to time, are popular.

In one field of inquiry there is absolutely no problem for conscientious young girls.

Every game of chance is beyond the pale of propriety. Any game in which gambling enters as a feature should be prohibited by one's conscience as well as by common consent on the part of decent people.

In the *House of Mirth*, the troubles which finally end in the pathetic death of Lily Bart begin with card playing for money. In order to pay her gambling debts, in themselves a deep disgrace, she recklessly borrows money from the husband of a friend and from that hour snares entangle her feet at every step. She is beautiful, tactful, a favorite in society, and she has opportunities surpassing most young women for happiness and yet her whole story is a tragedy. The custom that gradually has grown up in this country of playing cards by daylight, clubs for this amusement meeting in the morning or the afternoon, is foreign to the ideals of our republic. Out of this custom, too, has insensibly grown another—that of giving card parties to raise money for charity, for a hospital, for the relief of a poor family, or the endowment of an orphanage or an old ladies' home. Money for charity would much better be given outright than raised in a manner to which many thoughtful people very properly object. It is as well to make a firm stand here, refusing to compromise or to be drawn in ever so little into a situation which may, by and by, prove difficult and embarrassing. Never compromise with conscience and if you have the faintest doubt about anything in the line of recreation, remain outside on safe ground.

You see, do you not, that recreation is not the real end of life but only one of the side issues. Recreation should re-create our powers. We do not live to amuse or to be amused, but to do our work. While we are occupied with this we have not time to devote to those other things which are only meant for rest and refreshment.

There is a danger against which I would caution my girl friends. We are too self-conscious and sometimes too ready to impose our ideas insistently upon those who are older. My little correspondent and hundreds like her are not called upon to legislate for the town or the world, but primarily are to do what their convictions lead them to consider right for themselves. A girl gains nothing by forcing her views needlessly on her family and her schoolmates and friends in society.

The sweet unconsciousness of the lily that is white and fragrant and clean, the exquisite loveliness of the rose that makes beautiful the garden, are symbolic of what girls should be. The temptation to pull one's self apart, dissect one's motives, classify and label them, and to advertise one's superior goodness subtly attacks otherwise gentle and lovable girls. Of a young woman whose attainments are high and whose manners are well-bred, I heard the remark, "It is impossible to live with Hortense. She is not satisfied with being exacting about herself. She is exacting with those who are in no way connected with her. She makes me think," said the girl who was talking, "of the scribes and Pharisees. Hortense is a Pharisee."

The point of this criticism was well taken. The Pharisees were excellent men who devoted so much thought and energy to the minor details of the law, the tithes of mint, anise, and cumin that they completely lost the essential spirit of life. We must not fail to live up to our standard of the right in amusement as in everything else, but we must beware of talking about our goodness, our sincerity, and our discretion.

Talk evaporates and its effect is soon lost. Right conduct is the single thing that stands the test of time.

Into a city household that insensibly had parted with a portion of its faith in God came as a guest a young cousin, who had been brought up in a home of piety. Priscilla was a dainty maiden, full of grace, full of tact, full of the unsullied sweetness of a youth that had never known anything except the cloistered tranquillity of a household apart from the gay world. Before she left her mother's house, she was told that she might do as she thought best about mingling in the society she would find in the home of her kinswoman. "Nothing will be like what it is here," said her mother, "but I do not want you to feel hampered. Do or leave undone as you are directed every day by the One who guides our steps, if we ask Him to lead us." I could not begin to tell you how quiet yet how potential was the spell that came into every group of which Priscilla became a part. She did not preach, she was not a *poseur*, she never criticized, but as one of her cousins expressed it, "The atmosphere around her was so pure and the place where she stood seemed so fair and clean, that she made a fellow want to be better." She exerted the influence that a girl may, who in daily living, represents Christ.

A young girl should never seem to be reproving her elders, nor a guest take the attitude of criticism toward a hostess. The art of maintaining one's own resolution and yet hurting no one's feelings and giving no one an opening to disparagement is worth seeking, and is a valuable accomplishment. When you were a child you may have read the long series of the *Elsie* books, and if so, you have not forgotten how abominably disagreeable little Elsie was in presuming to be more virtuous than her father and other grown people.

Elsie was a tiresome little prig. To be vain and conceited is almost as bad as to be unreasonable and perverse. Charles Kingsley epitomized a volume in his familiar lines:

Be good, sweet maid, and let who will be clever;
Do noble things, not dream them all day long.
And so make life, love, and the great forever
One grand, sweet song.

I have been asked by evidently conscientious young women if I approve of raising money for church and charitable uses by means of lotteries, euchre parties, dances, and other amusements and means around which gathers no little objection in the minds of thoughtful people. I wish to say emphatically to girls that gambling in any phase or form is an insidious evil not to be tampered with, and that the use of the lottery, however veiled, is an inconsistent thing in Christian work. We cannot consider it consistent to subordinate religion to worldly amusements, even when they are in themselves innocent. Our contributions for church and charity should belong to that breaking of the alabaster box which sheds a sweet perfume around because it means self-denying love. When we combine a worldly amusement with our Christian giving, we serve ourselves first and our Lord second; we insult His cause and have no right to claim the blessing that He promises when He says, "Inasmuch as ye have done it to one of the least of these, ye have done it unto Me."

Chapter XVII

On the Road

WHENEVER we have in this country a great industrial exposition, attracting throngs of visitors, the railroads and steamboats offer special reductions by way of inducement to the traveling public. Stay-at-home people, who seldom venture far afield, are allured by these invitations and if father and mother cannot afford themselves the great pleasure of an outing, they try their best to let their young people go. They argue with a good deal of truth that such outings are educational and that if their Caroline or Jenny cannot go to Europe or the Far East, the next best thing will be to send them to a place which has the treasures of Europe and the Far East on exhibition.

A daughter is the home's most precious possession, and when she goes abroad alone she should be carefully safeguarded. Unscrupulous men and women have not in the past hesitated to lay traps for the ensnaring of innocent and unsuspecting girlhood, at centers to which the world comes. Part of the active beneficence of the Young Women's Christian Association has lately taken the form of Travelers' Aid work, so that no young girl arriving alone and unprotected at a railway terminal in a strange city need be without safe shelter, wise direction, and trustworthy friends.

If you are a country girl accustomed to the environment of a small community where everybody knows everybody else, and if you are obliged for the first time to take a long journey without escort, either to attend an exposition or fill a business situation in a city, you need have no timidity about your safety on the road. Having purchased your ticket and checked your trunk, you are in the care of the conductor and until you arrive at your destination he will show you all needed courtesy. Ask questions and seek information only of the uniformed officials of the road when you are traveling. Do not be uncivil, cold, or curt with fellow passengers and if occasion arises do not fear to show kindness to a mother accompanied by little children, to a young girl on her way to school, or anyone else who seems in want or need of a trifling attention. But beware of making friends with ingratiating strangers. No man young or old has the privilege of beginning a conversation with a young woman sitting by herself whom he does not know, and who does not know him. His doing this and above all his offering his visiting care is a gross impertinence.

Before leaving home, if a girl is not going immediately to friends and is not to be met on arrival at her destination by relatives, every arrangement should be made as to her place of boarding or lodging. This is easily done by means of a preliminary correspondence with the local Young Women's Christian Association. Should there by any chance be no association in the place to which she is going, her pastor will willingly write to a minister of her denomination in the town to which she is bound, and through him arrangements may be made for her going, without delay, to a home where she will be lonely, perhaps, but as safe as in her father's house. Never go in search of employment to a strange city without being furnished with letters of introduction and sufficient money to maintain yourself in comfort while looking for work.

Girls who have never been away from home are a little anxious about sleeping car accommodations and the like. A little observation will show them that there is nothing here to be dreaded. The necessary disrobing for the night is done behind the curtains which the porter lets down when, at the request of a passenger, he makes up her berth. There are little hammocks of netting which hold small articles and there is a receptacle at one end of the berth in which larger articles may be folded and placed. A loose kimono or long dressing sacque is worn in passing through the car to the dressing room appropriated to the use of women. A little patience is often requisite here, especially in the morning when people are making their toilets. The inconsiderate young woman arranges her hair and dresses for the day in a leisurely fashion, oblivious to the fact that her fellow passengers are awaiting their turn. The unselfish one makes what haste she may and is very careful to usurp no time that belongs to another.

If a girl does not desire to pay the prices of meals in a railway dining car, prices which are seldom other than expensive, she may provide herself with a dainty luncheon before leaving home. Our English cousins everywhere carry with them a tea basket and have the material for making the cups of tea in which they delight. If one is ill in the morning and cannot quickly become used to the motion of railway cars, a little fruit or a biscuit may tide her over the crucial moment.

In crossing the ocean the same qualities of forethought, consideration, and regard for others obtain as when traveling on land. It is not too much to say that a young gentlewoman armed with the delicate courtesy that belongs to good breeding may if need be make the circuit of the globe without once receiving an insult, finding herself in an awkward situation, or incurring any particular peril. Everywhere she will find men and women at her service, and kindness will be shown her in an unforeseen emergency.

If you are engaged in business and only have a short summer holiday and wish to spend it to the best possible advantage, you may go wherever you please limited only by the means at your disposal and have a rest time without embarrassment, let, or hindrance. If, however, you wish to stay at an inn at the seashore or in the mountains, you will have a much better vacation provided you go in company with two or three friends than if you go alone. A tired girl may reach a place where the only thing she can do is to spend her holiday in absolute inaction, lying in a hammock under the trees, or idling through the bright hours on a sunny veranda. It may be that she has seen so many people, waited on so many customers, footed up so many bills, and written so many letters that she feels a yearning desire to get away by herself. Her best choice will be to board at a farmhouse and nestle under the wing of a motherly woman who will give her three meals a day, and beyond this treat her with a little wholesome neglect.

If her holidays are few and far between a girl must get out of them and compress into them all the joy in existence that she possibly can. The working girl who is no drone in the busy hive is entitled to recreation and refreshment on the road. For her I crave in her summer vacation whatever will best fit her to take up her work again, and whatever will give her most of mental stimulus and physical repose, according as her want may be. All the more that her holiday is usually a short one, should it be a matter of conscientious prevision. She is entitled to the benefit that accrues from change of scene and cessation of monotony.

Most young women in business have loved ones to some extent dependent upon them. The saleswoman carries her salary home and hands it wholly or in part to her mother. The factory operative does the same. In cases where the working woman manages her own earnings she still appropriates a large share of them to a home—it may be in the town where she works, or in a distant state.

The trained nurse with her comparatively large honorarium is helping to pay for her brother's education, or to lift a mortgage from the home acres. The reporter has a mother to care for. Few among the young women who toil with their brains or their hands are able to lay aside very much for the rainy day, nor do they wish to evade obligations of affection that imply sacrifices borne for relatives and friends.

Every working girls' club and settlement carries through the year the thought or the plan of relaxation for the girls who spend social evenings within its doors. One of the best gifts any association of young women bestows on its members is not directly educational or directly philanthropic, but it has to do with making them happier on the road of life and providing them here and there with a rest when they are weary.

Another aspect of our manners on the road concerns our method of dealing with duty. We may or may not like the work we have to do. We may or may not be satisfied with circumstances. We may feel a conviction amounting almost to a certainty that we are worth more than we are paid. Interruptions of one or another kind may try our nerves. Nobody has immunity from annoyances and vexations in the life of business, and very likely they help in the discipline that makes us stronger and gentler.

A girl left home one morning for her post behind a counter in a great department store, and all the way downtown she was reflecting on the manifold miseries of her lot. She had risen at four to prepare breakfast for her father, who had to start before dawn in order to reach his place of employment. Her mother was ill and confined to her bed. As her mother was janitress in the apartment house where they lived, she was expected to keep the stairs and hallways clean. My little friend swept and scrubbed before she made herself tidy and set her face toward the shop where her day's duties would keep her on her feet for hours together. She was weary and spent when she left home, and discontent with her hard conditions made them no easier. In a half-desperate mood tinged with rebellion, she arranged her work and awaited her first customer. That customer happened to be a fragile old lady, a little lame, and very timid and hesitating in manner. The girl's heart relented as the dear old lady asked to be shown this and the other article, and she tried to serve her as well as she could. There flashed into her mind a text she had heard the Sunday before about "doing good as ye have opportunity." The text crept into her heart like a message from the Master this girl was humbly and reverently following. She applied it to each customer as the shop grew full and she was kept too busy to think about herself or her home. The morning slipped away; noon arrived with its respite for luncheon. The girl beside her was nearly blind with headache, and my friend told her to change turns and go first for her luncheon and walk in the fresh air. Meanwhile, on the other side of the counter stood a young woman richly gowned, with an air of prosperity in every line of her graceful figure, and with amiability and happiness written on her charming face. She made a trifling purchase and was about to go when suddenly she paused, noting the pallor and listlessness and the dark shadows and drooping mouth that indicated fatigue in the clerk who had waited on her. "You look very tired," she said. "Let me give you these." Swiftly she laid a great bunch of purple violets on the counter and was gone.

Here were two travelers on the road; one with every advantage and the other with every handicap. But each had a chance that day to carry out the Scripture injunction, "Be pitiful, be courteous."

The miles of a road leading from place to place and by and by bringing us to a mansion of endless rest and, too, of endless activity appeal to the thoughtful mind. We have to take only one step at a time. We need not trouble ourselves much about the morrow for our Savior has said that the morrow shall take thought for the things of itself. The present moment is ours. We may make it glad or sorrowful, fruitful or barren by the way in which we use it. F. W. Robertson has said, "It is not by change of circumstances, but by fitting our spirits to the circumstances in which God has placed us that we can be reconciled to life and duty." Suppose we begin each day by saying with Frances Ridley Havergal,

Take my hands and let them move
At the impulse of Thy love.

Take my feet and let them be
Swift and beautiful for Thee.

Take my intellect and use
Every power as Thou shalt choose.

The hardest bit of road undertaken in this spirit will shine in the light of God.

Rev. Dr. J. R. Miller, to whom we are indebted for many helpful messages and cheering words, tells us in one of his books the story of a boy who turned a hindrance into an advantage. The story may have its meaning for some girl who feels herself cruelly straightened on the road.

> There is no doubt that every hard thing that God permits to come into our life has a blessing wrapped up in it. The things which appear before us as discouragements prove to be helps toward nobler attainments. A Christian physician, whose career has been full of faith and noble ministry, gives this experience: He was a poor boy, and a cripple. One day he was watching some other boys on the ball field. They were active, strong, and wealthy. As he looked on his heart grew bitter with envy. A young man who stood beside him noted the discontent on his face, and said to him, "You wish you were in those boys' place, don't you?" "Yes, I do," was the answer. "I reckon God gave them money, education, and health," contin-

ued the young man, "to help them to be of some account in the world. Did it never strike you," he continued, after a moment's pause, "that he gave you your lame leg for the same reason,— to make a man of you?"

The boy gave no answer, and turned away. He was angry, but did not forget the words. His crippled leg God's gift! To teach him patience, courage, perseverance! To make a man of him! He thought of the words till he saw their meaning. They kindled hope and cheer, and he determined to conquer his hindrance. He grew heroic. He soon learned that what was true of his lame leg was true of all the difficulties, hindrances, and hard conditions of his life,—they were all God's gift to help him to be of some account in the world,—to make a man of him.

The lesson is for all of us, especially for young people who seem born with more than their share of disadvantages, limitations, hard conditions. God gave them this load, whatever it is, to make something of them. The deformity, the burden, the weight of someone's need laid upon the shoulder, the inheritance of difficulty which seems to be a hindrance to a worthy life is but another chance to grow, to become stronger, richer-hearted, more a man or a woman, to win a higher place in life, and a brighter crown in glory.

Chapter XVIII

Days of Illness

IN A LITTLE room fronting a long village street, a girl sits day after day beside the window, unable to take a step without assistance. Year in and year out in summer's heat and winter's cold her sweet face in the invalid's chair looks out on the passers-by. Often she cheerily waves her thin hand to someone she knows; often people turn in at the gate to leave her a book or a flower or to tell her what is happening and get for themselves a little of the sunshine she carries in her soul, and several times a week the postman stops at her door to leave the letters that her friends send her from distant places, in which she is remembered and loved.

God has laid upon this child of His a cross that to many would seem heavy, but which she accepts with a serenity and fortitude that make it light. When one bears a cross with patience and without complaint, it bears her. And beneath its weight her spirit rises into daily communion with Him who toiled up Calvary bearing His Cross.

This girl was as light of foot, as strong, as merry as any girl who reads these lines until one day an accident, apparently slight, removed her from the activities of the home and made her a captive shut in behind the bars of invalidism.

I do not know through what sacred experiences she was brought to her present condition of acquiescence and submission, and to a realization of the Savior's joy. But I know that He has been with her: "The dross to consume, and the gold to refine."

A young girl in the bloom of her early teens had the misfortune to be one day in a crowded building when the floor gave way, and a number of people were seriously hurt. She had been the gayest of the gay, fond of outdoor life, and a leader in everything that went on in her town. The girls did nothing of importance without consulting her. Suddenly, an arrest was laid on her freedom, her physical life fell under an eclipse, and for nearly five years she spent most of her time on a couch, seldom able to walk across the room. From this ordeal she finally recovered and regained her old vigor. But into her face during the time of shadow came a light that had been wanting before. She has been nobler and lovelier since the trial than she would have been but for its touch of tender discipline.

Much as we desire the perfection of health, and great as is the obligation to seek it, we must not overlook the fact that days of illness are appointed at times for God's dear children. One of the most intimate things in the wonderful life of Christ upon the earth is His sympathy with suffering, His compassion for the sick, and His constant ministry of healing. As He went from one little hamlet to another in Galilee or Judea, the cry would be raised, "Jesus of Nazareth passeth by," and whether someone reached out a timid finger and just caught the fringe of His garment's hem, or He entered a house and looked lovingly on someone tossing on a bed of pain, He brought with Him health and life. Into sickrooms Jesus came and He never went away without leaving a blessing. Of the aged woman or the young girl to whom the Lord brought new life it might be said,

He touched her hands and the fever left her.
Oh! we need His touch on our fevered hands;
The cool, still touch of the Man of Sorrows.
Who knows us and loves us, and understands.

It may be the fever of pain and anger,
When the wounded spirit is hard to bear,
And only the Lord can draw forth the arrows
Left carelessly, cruelly, rankling there.

Whatever the fever, His touch can heal it,
Whatever the tempest, His voice can still;
There is only one joy as we seek His pleasure;
There is only rest as we choose His will.

We must admit, however, that illness may be due to direct violation of God's laws. If this is the case and we bring it on ourselves by an act of sinful folly, we are as culpable as if we willfully indulge in ill-temper or stoop to untruth or speak unkindly of our neighbor. People have always understood this.

In Paul Leicester Ford's story "Janice Meredith," there is a little scene common enough a hundred years ago. But hardly to be paralleled in the twentieth century. A mother is helping her daughter dress and she relentlessly draws the laces of the girl's corset tighter and tighter in her effort to reduce the girl's waist to the slenderness then in vogue. Whether or not the girl could breathe without effort was of no consequence. She must have the accepted hourglass shape, and the waist that could be spanned by two hands, or her mother would suffer agonies of shame.

The willowy waists of our grandmothers in their youth explained their frequent fainting fits and their chronic ill health. They had no breathing room and this, added to repeated violations of hygienic laws, made them fragile and an easy prey to the white peril that used to ravage many fair homes.

Just after the Civil War, in a southern city, I met a young

woman who was fading away with consumption. A friend told me that this girl, in robust health three years earlier, had not only worn a cruelly tight corset in the daytime but for more than two years had slept in one every night in the determination to reduce the size of her waist. She succeeded, she became an invalid, and she died. In the latter part of the eighteenth century and the beginning of the nineteenth girls were seldom well and, as for their mothers, they took for granted colds and headache, rheumatism and other ills, and regarded them as among the necessary evils that had to be borne.

Marion Harland in an interesting paper on the life of Virginia in the forties recalls the delicacy of health which was accepted with resignation by the matrons in a county distinguished for wealth and comfort. As were the mothers, so were the daughters. Nobody expected to be well long at a time. Headaches were chronic and very few girls or women understood what perfect health meant.

We have learned that cause and effect are often linked together. The health rate of women has been raised since we have learned to live in accordance with those laws of God that govern the body. We have no right to lay the blame for any illness coming to us through our own heedlessness or folly at the door of divine providence. Preventable illness is one of those mistakes for which we ought to ask forgiveness on our knees. Everyone should recognize responsibility in the matter of keeping well if possible, and as long as possible, and everyone should remember that the will and the prevalent tone of thought have much to do in maintaining health. When contagious disease is in our neighborhood or our home we should do what we can to confine it within strict quarantine limits. The point for each of us is to fight illness by the aid of science and the help of the best physician within call, and to consider it a calamity and not a blessing except in disguise.

This, of course, does not apply to those who are ill

through no fault of theirs, and who must accept without murmur or complaint the lot appointed them. They belong with the saints and martyrs, who learn by God's grace to drink their cup of woe and be triumphant over pain.

Unbroken health is a good gift of God. Illness and suffering are also His gifts to some of us, and the way we bear them shows to the world the reality and worth of our belief in Christ.

A pretty little story is told about the mignonette and the gravel-walk. The gravel-walk said to the mignonette, "How fragrant you are today!"

"Yes," said the flower, "I have been trodden on."

"I am trodden on all day," said the gravel-walk, "but it does not make me sweet."

The mignonette answered, "That is a pity. The more I am bruised the more sweetness I can give."

In the parable is there not a lesson for us? Shall we not receive whatever God sends without a murmur, so that it may make us lovelier and dearer to those about us?

One use of suffering is to teach sympathy. If you have never known the torture of aching nerves, if you have had entire exemption from bodily pain, you will have no conception of what it means and perhaps will be impatient when it is present in the home, and have very little toleration for those who suffer.

You may never be a good nurse, for nurses are born as well as trained. But until you are yourself ill you will not feel the gratitude you ought to the woman who nurses you in illness. I, for one, never see a nurse in a hospital ward or in a home without a feeling of reverence and a thought that here is one of God's earthly angels ready to do His errands. The white cap, the spotless apron, the print dress compose a uniform that I respect. A girl who is looking for a career in which she may serve God and endure a good deal of hardship at the same time will find her opportunity in the work of the trained nurse. When dangerous illness invades a home, the nurse is as eagerly sought as the physician and is not less useful than he.

The presence of an invalid in a household is often a benefit to children and young people, who learn gentleness and self-restraint in their efforts to surround the dear one with comfort and quiet. The invalid's temptation against which she should guard is twofold. She may grow morbid and melancholy and indulge depression instead of making a gallant fight against its inroad, or she may drift into selfishness and by ceaseless small exactions wear out the strength of her caretakers. Unless one is suffering from a disease that makes her altogether helpless, she should do what she can for herself and save her friends from exertions that unduly tax them. She should refuse to take a gloomy view of the situation. A physician once said to me, "It is the nature of disease to get well," and nature, the wise old mother, has secrets of healing that she does not always impart to the medical profession. There may be a tomorrow of health for the girl who is ill today.

Nor should anyone who is ill be oblivious to the fact that some of the world's best work has been accomplished by people who were never very strong. The long series of exquisite pictures painted by Sir Edward Burne-Jones were the work of a man who was never robust, and who often had to strive against physical weakness and pain. Robert Louis Stevenson has left for all time a record so inspiring and so splendid of work done against odds that I copy it here for the encouragement of some invalid on whom the brave words may act like a tonic:

> For fourteen years I have not had a day's real health; I have wakened sick, and gone to bed weary; and I have done my work unflinchingly. I have written in bed, and written out of it, written in hemorrhages, written in sickness written torn by coughing, written when my head swam for weakness; and for so long, it seems to me I have won my wager and recovered my glove. I am better now, have been, rightly speaking, since first

> I came to the Pacific; and still, few are the days when I am not in some physical distress. And the battle goes on—ill or well, is a trifle; so as it goes. I was made for a contest, and the powers have so willed that my battlefield should be this dingy, inglorious one of the bed and the physic bottle.

All things considered an invalid is the gainer by not allowing herself to be entirely laid on the shelf. If there is anything that the hands can do, it is well that they should be employed. If the hands are cramped and useless, yet the brain may be active, and the invalid may direct or suggest where she cannot personally engage in a task. A household to which I was bound by ties of friendship was for years controlled and guided by a woman who never rose from her bed, who was nursed night and day and who kept her poor hands under the coverlet lest the sight of them should give others pain. Yet no house in a large city was better managed than was hers; servants remained with her for years performing their duties with fidelity. She directed the education of her only child, seeing his teachers, retaining his confidence, welcoming him and his boyfriends into her room with smiles so bright that they loved to come there, and never for an instant yielding her soul's strength to the demands of a body often racked by severe pain.

The invalid's room should be a sanctuary. Think that God must love you very much to take with you the pains He does to make you beautiful, gentle, and patient. Think, too, that life for all of us is lived only one day at a time. Think nothing about the future. Live hour by hour, sure that God can give you strength and endurance for one step more. A day is coming when the trial will be over and you will forever be done with everything that belongs to sorrow and suffering. In the heaven to which God's children are going there is no more pain. In that land the inhabitant shall never say, "I am sick."

Chapter XIX

About Conversation

GIRLS sometimes complain that they have no art in conversation. They say, "Do tell us how to talk." To hear a group of girls merrily chattering, the gay sallies punctuated by bursts of happy laughter, one would not imagine that they found much difficulty in this particular line. Yet chatter is not conversation. The art of talking agreeably and well is an art worth cultivating.

Did you ever notice that you talk with some people without the slightest effort, that words come to you quickly, ideas throng, and you have no trouble whatever in expressing your meaning? In other company you are very likely tongue-tied. One of the most brilliant talkers I ever met shuts up like a clam in some society: his lips are sealed, his countenance is blank, he literally has nothing to say. Something to say is imperative if one is to talk well. There are people who monopolize conversation. They have plenty to say and they like to have the floor. In fact, they bear down opposition by the impetuous quality of their rhetoric and when they are present nobody else has the ghost of a chance.

Sydney Smith once wrote to a friend after dining with Lord Macaulay that there had been an agreeable surprise about the latter's talk: flashes of silence. Conversation is a sort of commerce. It should never be one-sided. At its best it is like a game, sometimes played by girls in which grace-hoops are tossed back and forth and caught by the partners in the game. One cannot expect that young girls on the threshold of their social existence shall be adepts in repartee, or that they shall shine in conversation. At this stage of their progress it is very much better that they should learn how to listen well. A good talker is not always popular, but a sympathetic listener is beloved in any company.

When older people are present, girls should not push to the front nor take a conspicuous place in general talk. When addressed they should be ready with an answer, but it is to the last degree disconcerting to see a very young girl occupying the center of the stage, using up the time, and volubly relating what has happened to herself or insisting upon her views while older people are compelled to be silent.

I remember a girl who was very attractive, very much at ease, very graceful and charming, but who antagonized everybody by this defect. "Where on earth did that child come from? Who are her people? What sort of mother has she?" inquired a whimsical old gentleman at the close of an evening when Sophie had successfully occupied the time, talked on every subject introduced, and left no opportunity for anyone but herself so much as to speak. As she took her courteous leave and sailed out of the room and out of the house, in the glory of her triumphant twenty years, a hush fell upon the drawing room and then everybody drew a breath of relief. Fireworks are dazzling, but they grow fatiguing. No young woman of twenty is expected to take and keep the lead in conversation in mixed company, at least half of which is composed of people very much older than she.

On the other hand, a girl of this age who listens

respectfully and intelligently, puts in a word here and there, and uses moderation in her own talk fills acceptably the role of girlhood in society. A girl is not expected to preach.

When girls are talking together on themes that enlist their interest they are seldom at a loss. Indeed, they need to be on their guard if in public places against speaking too loudly and introducing the names of their friends. This latter mistake is far too common. This is a little world, and you may mention the name of an acquaintance in a ferryboat or on the deck of a steamer or in a railway car, and her first cousin whom you have never seen may be sitting directly opposite you hearing every word. You may say nothing ill-natured and yet you would find it embarrassing should the incident be described to your absent friend. Two acquaintances of mine met in Berlin, casually, and fell into conversation about friends at home, mentioning in passing an engagement that was about to be announced in a little western town in America. Turning, the first person they saw proved to be a brother of the lady whose name they had mentioned, and whom they supposed to be three thousand miles away. Some years ago it was freely related in diplomatic circles that a man, who had filled various offices creditably at home and abroad, lost the appointment he anticipated as minister in an important foreign capital because he thoughtlessly mentioned a name in conversation with a friend at a reception in the White House. The remark he made was overheard, maliciously repeated, and interrupted—if it did not end—a brilliant political career.

To be on one's guard in talking about people and particularly about the living is an excellent rule. Too much of the staple of conversation consists of gossip about persons we know or persons who are known to our friends. Great statesmen, great poets and painters, great commanders, women eminent for good deeds and the like may be talked about freely. But we should not discuss our friends, their foibles or their peculiarities. If a girl has a gift of mimicry, she should be more than careful how and when she exercises it lest she wound sensitive feelings and inflict pain.

Another conversational error is the setting of people right about unimportant matters. You may be very sure that your friend is wrong as to date or a place of an incident. But unless some essential difficulty will be created by letting some of the misstatement go, it is wise to refrain from a correction. It should go without saying that we do not interrupt our friends or rudely rush in with our speeches before they have finished theirs. Should a friend hesitate for a word do not supply it, but wait patiently until he or she succeeds in finding the word sought. I saw a beautiful instance of this courtesy in a company where a very old man, long past eighty, was talking to a group of younger people. He had been in his day a wonderful scholar and orator and a social leader, but the clouds were gathering over him and mind and memory had been weakened. In the midst of a sentence it seemed as if a curtain dropped in his brain. He stopped, was silent, and could not get the word he wanted. No one gave it to him. Everyone waited with utmost quietness and presently the curtain rolled up again, the word came and he completed what he had begun to say. The temptation is often almost irresistible to supply what one supposes to be the missing word. Yet usually it is the kinder part not to yield to it.

Conversation is defaced by slang and by all catchwords that border ever so remotely on profanity. Girls at school are very apt to fall into what I may call the habit of italics. They underscore their words and drop into the superlative on slight occasion. It is easy to say that conversation would be colorless were we always literal. Yet nothing is gained by bringing words of large import such as awful and terrible and horrible into relations where they do not belong. As for such exclamations as "Heavens and earth," "Goodness," "My land," "Great Scott," and other needless interpolations, they are excrescences on polite speech and ought not to be tolerated.

A girl often hears what may be called picturesque current slang from her brothers and their friends. But as she owes it to the family and the community to acknowledge her duty to her mother tongue, she should not adopt it in her conversation.

One learns to talk well as one learns to read, to write, or to swim, to play the mandolin, or the harp: by daily practice. If we suffer ourselves to fall into heedless mannerisms, to drop our final g's, to mispronounce, or to use the words that do not nicely express our thought we shall never be good talkers. There is very great difference among girls as to vocabulary. A good vocabulary that enables one to select the best word, that helps one to choose between words, and that furnishes one with metaphor and simile is gained perhaps by reading rather than by talking. If you read good books and grow familiar with the style of the best authors, you will, without having to strive for it, use good English in your conversation.

Another point that is helpful is acquaintance with what is going on in the world. Part of every girl's education should be a course in reading the newspapers. We are living in a time that is of absorbing interest and intensely rapid movement. Things are happening every day. We cannot take up a morning paper without discovering that the world has advanced since yesterday. In reading the paper do not confine yourselves to the accidents and crimes, to the reports of the smart set, or the new styles in fashion but read about the things that are changing the map of the world: the great wars, the great revolutions, the new inventions, the wave marks of human progress. No girl who reads the newspapers intelligently will fail to be able to take her part in ordinary conversation. Women confine themselves, it is said, too much to trivialities, to the faults of servants, the disappointments of dressmakers, and the little things that are of small account in daily life. Men, on the contrary, talk of bigger things and one reason may be that men usually know by much reading of the newspapers what is happening in the world. If you do not care for the newspapers, then I advise you to read Shakespeare and Milton. Is there anywhere a girl who tells me that she cannot become interested in these magnificent writers? who saw so much and sounded so deeply in the story of humanity? I can only say that I hope her limitation is due to her youth and that she will change her point of view after a while. If she ever aspires to converse admirably she must have culture. Real culture is the background of good conversation.

At one time when Charles Dickens was more widely read than he now is his characters entered freely into the common talk of the day. People met one another and spoke of Mr. and Mrs. Boffin, Tommy Traddles, Dora Copperfield, Betsey Trotwood, Susan Nipper, Mr. Micawber, old Scrooge, Paul Dombey, and little Dorrit as if they were veritable flesh-and-blood characters and not puppets on the stage. Thackeray's people never took so strong a hold on the popular imagination, although Colonel Newcomb, Becky Sharp, and Henry Esmond were frequently alluded to in cultivated talk.

A certain familiarity with standard literature and particularly with the best writers of English will help you very much in conversation.

I may not be amiss to remind my girl readers that the quality of the voice is an almost unerring index to refinement or the reverse. Shakespeare tells us that a low voice is an excellent thing in woman. A low voice provided it be clear, and free from the habits of losing itself at the end of a sentence is a distinctly attractive and advantageous possession. It is much more important to speak with precision, letting every word fall from the lips clean and clear-cut as a new coin, than to speak loudly or with overemphasis. In some parts of our country the letter R is too prominent; in others it is almost eliminated from speech. Provincialisms of every kind are to be avoided. If one is talking with the deaf there will be great success in reaching the ear that is dulled if one speak slowly and distinctly in a voice not over loud, than if one shout.

The good conversationalist is at pains to exclude no one from the magic circle of the talk. Should an elderly or invalid friend be present a girl will try unobtrusively to bring him or her into the charmed region of pleasant and informal talk. Private conversations are not permissible in rooms where the family and friends are assembled.

Chapter XX

What to Wear

"THINK OF IT!" said Evelyn, laying down a morning newspaper with a sigh. "There is one girl in this land who has everything she wants: furs of silver fox from her head to her feet, a long stole to the hem of her dress, a great flat muff for her hands, and a lovely toque for her head. She is having several broadcloth gowns made at once, as well as others for her trousseau, and she even has had a tint called after her, the Alice Blue."

"For my part," said I, with a loving look at Evelyn's earnest face, "I should not envy the young lady you speak of the trouble and toil of so many fittings. A girl who is getting a number of beautiful gowns made simultaneously has to go through considerable fatigue under the hands of her dress-maker, and as for the tint you speak of, the Evelyn blue as I see it in a certain person's eyes is good enough for me. As for the furs they are no doubt extremely elegant, but that little set of yours is quite as useful in protecting you from the cold and has the grace of matching any costume you may happen to wear."

"That's very well," Evelyn replied. "These squirrel furs are warm and are pretty, and I'm glad I have them, but now and then I can't help dreaming how nice it would be to have ermine and sable and mink and silver fox and sealskin as if I were a princess royal, or the daughter of an American president just about to be married to an American who has no doubt millions to his credit. How I should enjoy having closets full of clothes, some of satin, others of silk or of soft crepe de Chine, beautiful gowns of wool, exquisite laces, and jewels of different kinds to set them all off."

"You fancy you would find complete satisfaction in such a wardrobe, my dear, but it would be no end of care and your maid would fall heir to many of the garments before they were half worn out. Only one gown, one set of jewels, one cape and muff may be worn by a young woman at one time. The rest are put away in the dark, must be kept from the dust and the moth, and generally cared for. As for the daughters of royal houses, they often are compelled to exercise an economy that would amaze American girls. Before the beautiful Alexandra became the bride of the Prince of Wales, now King Edward the Seventh, she paid a visit to Queen Victoria. About that time there was a fashion of skirts and jackets, the latter worn over a silk of muslin waist. The little Danish princess had not many skirts, but she had a variety of jackets. One day the queen said to her, 'What a fancy you seem to have for jackets, my dear.'

" 'Oh,' said Alexandra, 'my sister and I make everything we wear and we can have more changes with jackets than without. They are not hard to make, and they do not cost much money.' "

Evelyn was silent a moment, then she glanced at the clock. "I shall just have time to reach Louise Haven's house by four o'clock," she said, "if I make haste. I am giving music lessons to Louise and her sister Jean. I do believe you are right. I have had a great deal of enjoyment out of the simple clothes I have bought and paid for since I began to earn money for myself. It is such a comfort not to be a burden in that way on my father."

As the door closed behind her I reflected on her last words. It is natural that young girls should take an interest in dress. It is a comfort, is it not, to save one's father expense?

"I would that beauty should go beautifully," says Tennyson, but his portrait of Enid in her faded silk lingers in our memory longer than any other word-painting in his gallery of maidens fair.

Girls themselves are so bewitching that they need less to enhance their charm than older women do. The color is in their cheeks and eyes and lips. The light is in their faces, the radiance of the springtime and the dawning is theirs. What a girl needs in dress is primarily fitness for the occasion. A working dress whether for the kitchen, the office or the shop, the artist's studio or the schoolroom should be trim, neat, well-fitting and free from superfluous decoration. The skirt should be short enough fully to clear the ground, the waist of washable material, and the fabric chosen with a view to service for housework and indoor use; something that may emerge from the tub in periodical freshness is preferable to mohair or cloth. If a girl's work is teaching, typewriting, or selling goods a cloth skirt lasts longer and looks better than muslins and prints and has a grace of adaptation surpassing them. In offices and shops, black is the favorite choice because it is modest and unobtrusive and may be relieved by white turnovers at the neck and wrists.

A girl who goes about a great deal in society requires a different outfit from that which serves the schoolgirl or the wage earner. The latter is amply provided for if in addition to her everyday dress she has one pretty tailor-made costume for church and visiting, a costume not necessarily expensive but severe and carefully made. The girl whose place in life is that of privilege and luxury, who has continual and shifting engagements at luncheons, teas, receptions, and dinners must have toilettes suitable for special occasions. If, as often happens, she finds it necessary to study ways and means, she may serve her purpose with a few things carefully selected and in good taste. A gown with two waists of soft gray, pure white, or rich black is a friend in need to such a girl. A handsome skirt with one high and one low waist, another dress suitable for church and for receptions, and one or two extra waists make a sufficient outfit for a girl and save her from embarrassment, let her invitations and engagements be ever so numerous. The present fashion of wearing shirtwaists of muslin, linen, or flannel as the season may indicate is one equally convenient for all girls; as suitable and becoming to the girl in an avenue mansion as to her friend in the tenement.

No girl looks ill-dressed in an immaculate shirtwaist, a well-cut skirt, and a simple jacket.

Dress should never be allowed to become a subject of anxiety on account of its expense. Only brainless and silly girls wish to wear clothing that advertises them as extravagant and showy, and which is obviously beyond their income or the means of their parents.

A good deal of attention is paid by those who have made dress a subject of study to shoes, stockings, and gloves. The effect of the finest clothing is marred by slipshod footgear and ill-fitting and unmended gloves. Hats, of course, are much in evidence. Avoid extremes in millinery. There are always simple shapes that suit youth and have the merit of finishing appropriately a youthful toilette.

Mrs. Oliphant in her autobiography tells us that her mother took special pains to make for her in her childhood the daintiest possible underclothing: the finest linen, the most delicate needlework were lavished by the Scottish mother on her little daughter's undergarments.

I was similarly drilled in my girlhood by a most fastidious mother. She would say, "Never mind very much about the outside dress, but have everything that is out of sight and what you wear next to the skin as fine and good as possible."

In working among the daughters of poverty I have often found that they needed a caution on this point. I have seen a young girl, whose weekly earnings amounted to five or six dollars and who out of that sum had to give some help to her family, dressed so far as hat, skirt, and jacket were concerned in a manner that indicated little economy. People have said to me that they looked at a gathering of factory girls, girls who worked hard and were paid little, "How can they afford to dress so well?" Sometimes, though not always, they dress as they do at the sacrifice of much that is womanly and dainty. More than once I have ascertained that there were rags and tatters beneath the fine dress, and sometimes when a girl has been taken ill and laid aside for weeks, she has not had so much as a decent nightdress. Here is opportunity for the fortunate girl to help her sister whose ways of life lie among the toilers. By suggestion, by example, and by simplicity in street dress the one girl may do much to elevate the taste and raise the standard of the other. In the ethics of dress a high place should be given to my mother's maxim, "Bestow most care on that which is out of sight."

Jewelry and ornament should be sparingly worn by young girls and they should if dependent on themselves set their faces like a flint against all buying on the installment plan. Diamonds on credit are a delusion and a snare. Imitation diamonds are unspeakably vulgar. The only realm in dress in which imitation goods are pardonable is the realm of lace. The priceless handmade laces are only for people of large wealth but there are beautiful laces made by machine which can hardly be called imitation, being a legitimate product of the loom, and they form as exquisite a garniture as the more costly kind, which may descend in a family from mother to daughter as an heirloom.

A great deal of latitude is at present allowed in the wearing of mourning. When one has lost a dear relative, it is a tribute to grief, a sign of respect to the memory of the dead, and a protection from social invitations to assume a mourning dress. The custom, however, is not universal and one suffers from no criticism if one continues to wear colors after a bereavement as before. No one should add to the gloom of the world by enveloping herself in the deep folds of smothering crêpe. The fashion is wasteful of money, detrimental to health, and intensely melancholy in the eyes of onlookers, as well as depressing to those who thus garb themselves and go walking about as moving monuments of woe. Simplicity in mourning is in better taste than too great elaboration. It should not be worn too long. Girls sometimes write, anxiously, asking questions on this point of someone who they suppose may be an authority. In this short life six months suffice as a term for the deepest mourning, and as a rule it should be laid off at the end of twelve months.

You may be interested to know that in novels written by women dress is more frequently a subject of allusion than in those written by men. The latter seldom enter into much detail, contenting themselves with splashes of color and broad effects, and not infrequently making amusing mistakes in the way they dress their heroines. Looking back to the eighteenth century we do not find that girls were dressed as they now are with a view to going out-of-doors in all weathers. One of Miss Austen's charming girls has a distressing sore throat in consequence of a walk in the rain taken in thin shoes, such as no girl of today would wear on the road at all. Tramping through woods and groves was hardly possible when shoes had paper soles and French heels. Charlotte Bronte's girls are usually dressed in sheer muslin, and they too have the thinnest shoes.

Robert Louis Stevenson in *David Balfour* describes the bewitching Highland maiden Katriona as he first saw her.

> There can nothing pass in the streets of a city without some following of idle folk and children. It was so now; but the more

> part melted away incontinent until but three were left. One was a girl; she was dressed like a lady, and had a screen of the Drummond colors on her head; but her comrades or (I should say) followers were ragged gillies, such as I had seen the matches of by the dozen in my Highland journey. They all spoke together earnestly in Gaelic, the sound of which was pleasant in my ears for the sake of Alan; and though the rain was by again, and my porter plucked at me to be going, I even drew nearer where they were, to listen.
>
> It chanced the girl turned suddenly about, so that I saw her face for the first time. There is no greater wonder than the way the face of a young woman fits in a man's mind, and stays there, and he could never tell you why; it just seemed it was the thing he wanted. She had wonderful bright eyes like stars, and I dare say the eyes had a part in it; but what I remember the most clearly was the way her lips were a trifle open as she turned. And whatever was the cause, I stood there staring like a fool.

You observe here the expression "dressed like a lady," the only part of the dress which the novelist singles out as a feature being a Drummond plaid. But he dwells with emphasis on the wonderful eyes like stars. This is the way it has been from the beginning. A man's attention is riveted not on a girl's dress but on a girl's self. A woman, on the contrary, sees everything another wears at a cursory glance, from the feather on her hat to the buckle on her shoes.

Dorothy Quincy once said pithily that the consciousness of being well dressed in some circumstances gave one a moral support that even religion might fail to give. The same acute critic of women remarked that she could never forgive a girl who was not well dressed or one who seemed to be pleased with her dress. There is a stratum of truth in both observations. When we are dressed as we ought to be we can go on with other things and think no more about our looks. It is very confusing to be disturbed over one's looks. If the mirror assures us that we are rightly equipped for a situation, we may dismiss that matter from our minds. To act as if pleased with ourselves is to preen like the peacock, the bird of vanity, yet the peacock is a male. The birds set us good examples: no female bird is seen strutting about with complacent airs as to feathers and crest.

Chapter XXI

The Writing Talent

THE WRITING TALENT is not the only talent that awakens envy and makes people regard its possessor as having been fortunate from the cradle. A marked originality and an extraordinary facility in any line of work and human endeavor are gifts that one thanks one's fairy godmother for leaving at one's door. The singing talent, the talent for painting, the talent for instrumental music bringing from organ and piano their hidden messages, and the talent for imparting instruction to little children or older students are talents that repay cultivation and add to the wealth of the age.

The writing talent is the one most longed for, most abused, and least understood. Here and there a girl is born with the faculty of insight and the power to paint in words the thing she sees or dreams. If this divine gift is hers by nature, training will do as much for it as it does for the artist in any other department of creative work. If it was not born in her, no amount of strenuous application or scholastic training will give it so far as its highest developments are concerned. Advertisements exploit the claims of certain schools and professors who undertake to teach young people how to write short stories and romances and poetry, and having written them, how to find a market for their sale. Girls, poets are born, not made. Story writing cannot be taught to anyone who does not have stories in her brain, who does not discern them in the firelight on the hearth and the starlight in the sky, and who cannot invest the everyday world with a halo of romance.

Mrs. Oliphant, during a long life of much sorrow and hardship, wrote poetry, stories, romances, biography, and criticism, kept the wolf from her door by the versatile pen and cared for as only a gifted and noble woman could, a number of very helpless people. Louisa Alcott, in a girlhood of bravery and splendid fortitude, unsurpassed in American annuals, wrote stories and stories and stories. In the intervals of her writing she sewed. She shrank from no task and no drudgery. She paid the debts of an impecunious philosophizing father, educated a younger sister, and did no end of excellent work endearing herself incidentally to girls in her *Little Women, Eight Cousins,* and *Rose in Bloom,* and she died before she had grown old. In her the writing talent was born. Inspiration came to her from common things and the spur of necessity compelled her to forge ahead.

Lucy Larcom, working as a factory girl in Lowell, Massachusetts, had the writing talent and it transformed her life. It must be in one to begin with and it cannot be imported from outside. An American novelist who has attained both wealth and fame, as a child was able to attend school irregularly and picked up her education by fragmentary reading and by a keen, quiet, almost unconscious observation of the village life around her. One day a neighbor came in and casually remarked that a prize had been offered by a newspaper for the best story to suit an occasion. When the neighbor went away the girl looked up from the book she was reading and said, "I wonder if I could write a story and send it in to compete for that prize?"

"Why not?" said a friend. The story was duly written and duly sent and it gained the prize, and that first small success encouraged the young writer to go on.

Another girl whose first novel had an instantaneous success used to spend hours of daylight completely lost in the books of her father's library. It was a library rich in standard authors and especially in history. The girl sat curled up in an easy chair and lived in feudal times, in early colonial days, in the thrilling scenes of the past and her own active creative imagination made it easy for her after a while to reincarnate old characters making them vital and dramatic, and to set upon the stage a moving panorama that held the eyes of all who gazed on its rapidly shifting situations. One of these girls was born in New England and the other in Virginia; each had the writing talent and owed almost nothing to schools and schoolmasters.

If you have this talent do not let anyone discourage you by the assertion that twenty-nine out of thirty youthful aspirants fail to gain a hearing, and that only the thirtieth succeeds. Why may you not be the thirtieth? Publishers are far more anxious to discover new writers than to bring out the work of those whose place is established. The world clamors for the new sensation. The writer whose name is known and whose powers have been accurately gauged has no particular advantage over the novice, who may be the greatest writer of the century.

Girls constantly inquire, How am I to be sure that the editor of this or that magazine will read what I send? The editor, poor man, comes in for a great deal of blame that he does not deserve. Whether he reads at first hand the manuscripts that are sent him or employs a professional expert to winnow and sift and select for him, of one thing you may be sure, and it is this: Good work is never rejected without being read. As the monthly magazines appear only twelve times a year and the weekly papers only fifty-two times a year and a great deal more by way of contribution from volunteers is offered than they can possibly print, you must take it for granted, if you fail, that you did not send precisely what they were in great need of. But you may be equally sure that what you sent received attention.

Although one may have the writing talent, one cannot depend on succeeding in authorship without an enormous amount of very hard work. No one ever had this talent in a more extraordinary degree than Robert Louis Stevenson. It is worth the while of any ambitious and clever girl to read in Stevenson's *Life and Essays* the methods he pursued in his own training. No one will ever write well who does not read and study wisely and sympathetically. Style is gained far less by writing than by reading. Much reading of great books forms a good style. Granted that you have thoughts of your own and some originality, you must still acquire the art of using language forcibly and directly, you must know how to find a dress for your thought, and you must gain a rich and copious vocabulary by acquaintance with the masterpieces of literature. Avoid insincerity in reading. Read books that tax your powers of attention, but never pretend to enjoy books for the shallow reason that somebody tells you they are the books you ought to like.

Journalism is a field of literature that offers inviting possibilities to girls who do not possess the creative faculty and who may never produce works of imagination, but who may learn to write intelligently about current events, and who may describe what they see, tell about fashions, or write paragraphs in which local color predominates. The work is not easy. It requires a capital of physical health, nerves that are not readily disturbed, and a fund of common sense. The girl reporter on daily papers of good standing is seldom assigned to duties unfit for a young woman's attention. The managing editor of a great daily has a fatherly or brotherly care for the young women on his staff, and he does not expect of them impossibilities or wish them thrust into situations of personal peril. But they must obey orders, they must be alert, tireless, swift, and always on time. A girl who would succeed as a newspaper woman must possess an all-round facility for work and must not think of herself first, but must put herself in the background and her task in the foreground. It is out of the question to do good work if one thinks primarily of the money it will bring, and yet it is true that the need of a pair of new shoes is a great incentive to doing one's best.

Singularly, three-fourths of the girls who think they can write confidently anticipate making a brilliant success in the department of reviewing books. I have seen a girl just out of college serenely sure that her equipment fitted her to cope with this difficult branch of writing, and have in my own mind suffered not a little over the disappointment that lay before her. Asked what sort of book she felt able to review, with a toss of her pretty head she replied that it did not matter. In her youthful self-confidence she was ready to attack psychology, political economy, history, science, romance, anything whatever if only the books might be put at her disposal. To review a book with fairness to the author, the theme, and the public is no light undertaking and can be carried through creditably only by a person who has some experience of life, some experience of books, and some acquaintance with the public needs and tastes, and the literary trend of the hour. Much of this is beyond the depth of a girl whose writing along critical lines has thus far been confined to papers in her composition class and her graduating thesis.

Those essayists who are most successful in book reviewing have been men and women of varied culture and profound learning. To this they have added charm of manner and felicitous diction and theirs have been in no small measure the happy accomplishment of finding without difficulty the appropriate phrase. Augustine Birrell, Henry van Dyke, Hamilton Wright Mabie, and others occur in this connection and a little schoolgirl cannot expect instant success if she enters the lists with them.

Nevertheless, if you will put the idea of publication entirely out of your mind and simply write for the pleasure of the thing and the intellectual profit to be derived from it, willingly giving time to apprenticeship that you may learn your trade, I advise you to review books. Read, mark, and inwardly digest good books. Indulge a catholic taste. Read whatever attracts you. Keep beside you a commonplace book, and copy passages that you admire. Steep yourself in your favorite author. If you are in earnest you will not grudge hours spent in reading and study. Review for your own sake, making a careful analysis and thoughtful comments that shall be strictly private, every strong book that comes in your way. Begin to accumulate a personal library. Buy, one by one, books that bear many readings. Ephemeral productions to be read and forgotten are not for the investment of a schoolgirl's purse. There are books well worth owning, and well worth self-denial that they may be purchased. I do not advise the lavishing of money on bindings and paper, on first editions, or editions deluxe. But, on the other hand, I have little patience with cheap reprints, poor paper, and flimsy bindings. A girl should consider well the books she buys, especially if she is a girl inclined to authorship, and she will discover in the end that money is not thrown away when spent on well-bound, well-printed, and well-appearing books.

If I counsel you to read Milton and Shakespeare, and above all other books the English Bible, do not pass the advice over as if it were perfunctory. If you cannot awaken in yourself an interest in these grandest of books, I fear you have not the talent that will one day bear fruitage in such writing as you long to do. One does not read the Bible only on account of its literary character, its magnificent affluence of poetry, its wonderful story of God's intense and vigilant love of and care for His children. One reads it because it is The Book to guide from earth to heaven. Yet no one can read the Bible daily, diligently, and lovingly without feeling its tremendous influence on style. It permeates Stevenson as it permeated Carlyle, it makes the charm of Barrie and Ian MacLaren, it is everywhere interfused with the very warp and woof of Rudyard Kipling. It colors the artistic work of Dante, Gabriel, Rossetti, and Sir Edward Burne-Jones and it thrills and vibrates in the pages of Ruskin, Tennyson, and Robert Browning. When I am confronted with a general neglect of the Bible on the part of young literary men and women of the moment I need no prophetic vision to show me that their work, however clever, however successful as a record of passing impressions, will be transient. No one who possesses the writing talent need anticipate much success in its cultivation unless she is prepared to devote thought and study and reverent reading to the Bible. Next to the Bible let her read Shakespeare, drinking deep draughts from his well of concise, vivid, and picturesque English.

One word more: If you are ever to make your mark in literature granting that you succeed in making a beginning, do not despise day labor. Do not undervalue drudgery. Rise to an independence of moods. The writer who scores a success in this period of tremendous competition and rapid pace must stick to her desk and do her day's work as conscientiously and regularly as if she were paid by the hour to work in a department store or a factory and must put aside invitations that invade her working time. Anthony Trollope, whose books are worth anyone's reading although their realism is occupied with a somewhat restricted social phase, used to write day in and day out, on the train, at friends' houses, or wherever he happened to be his accustomed stint of one thousand words an hour. This was swift work but it was not hurried for he used the pen of a master. Hurry and worry ruin work.

Will you pardon me, my little friend whose head is running over with bright fancies, if I whisper in your ear that when you write you must not forget the trifling details of punctuation and spelling? May I remind you that manuscripts should be sent flat, not rolled, to a publisher, should be written on one side of the paper only, with black ink, in a legible hand, or that still better they should be typewritten? Wherever sent they should be accompanied by your real name and post-office address in the same, not in a separate enclosure, and stamps for return postage in the event of their being declined, accompany them. Even genius cannot ordinarily afford to overlook these little details when manuscripts are sent from the loving hands of their writers to win their way in a world of strangers.

A girl who feels that she can be happy only if she gratifies her desire to write must not let herself be daunted by rebuffs at the outset. There are men and women at the top of the ladder today who had a hard struggle before they gained the first foothold and began their steady climb. Set the right value on perseverance, but do not hope if you have no other resource, very soon or very certainly to earn a livelihood in literature. It is the bread-winning profession of the few. The many would far better attempt almost anything else if the comforts and luxuries of life for themselves and their dear ones are to depend on what they gain by the pen.

Do you like Kipling's lilting verse? Here is a poem of his that sings itself over in my thoughts as I finish this chapter:

When Earth's last picture is painted, and the tubes
are twisted and dried,
When the oldest colors have faded, and the youngest
critic has died,
We shall rest, and, faith, we shall need it—lie down
for an aeon or two,

Till the Master of All Good Workmen shall set us
to work anew!

And those that were good shall be happy; they shall
sit in a golden chair;
They shall splash at a ten-league canvas with brushes
of comet's hair;
They shall find real saints to draw from—Magdalene,
Peter and Paul;
They shall work for an age at a sitting and never be
tired at all!

And only the Master shall praise us, and only the
Master shall blame;
And no one shall work for money, and no one
shall work for fame;
But each for the joy of the working, and each,
in his separate star,
Shall draw the Thing as he sees It for the
God of Things as They Are.

Chapter XXII

The Motherless Girl

ON THE EVE of a daughter's marriage a mother said to me, "I shall miss Mary more than I can tell. She and I have been such friends."

When mother and daughter are congenial the relation between them is that of the most intimate and confidential friendship. We often notice as girls grow up a sort of sympathetic understanding between them and their mothers that makes the tie not unlike that which unites sisters. The daughter in a way is the mother's second self. In her sweet face the mother has a vision of her own vanished girlhood. A few years more or less do not make a woman old, and a mother often feels as young as the daughter by her side. Indeed, there is a moment in girlhood when most girls feel anything but young. To their own consciousness they carry a good deal of weight, and one may sometimes meet the contrast in the home of a lighthearted mother and a grave caretaking daughter, who might almost change places.

However this may be, there is in the bond a deep, sweet opportunity for friendship that is found in precisely that form nowhere else.

Living under the same roof the two have much in

common. If the family is large and the daughter one of the elder children, she early shares her mother's solicitude and halves her burdens. A child in such a family runs to the elder sister for comfort and help just as to the mother, and the mother if compelled to leave home for a season feels very safe in committing responsibility to one who will neglect no trust. They have little secrets together, little jests, a stock of associations that are their own. Gradually, the sheath of childhood has slipped away from the maiden and she to her mother is another woman, the truest, dearest, and closest of friends.

When a girl has the great misfortune to lose her mother in infancy and during the first ten years of life, a whole world of sweetness and joy is forever taken from her. The bereavement is so great that words cannot measure it. There will never be a year of all the years when she will not need love, counsel, suggestion, and aid that her mother would have given her lavishly and that no one on earth can give in the same degree. A father will do his best, but he cannot enter into some regions of a daughter's life. If a girl has grown into the brightness and bloom of the later teens before her mother is taken away she appreciates her loss more thoroughly and realizes more profoundly her loneliness and desolation, but as time passes she will realize also that during the most important period of life her mother's molding hand helped to shape her character.

Undoubtedly, in numerous instances a second mother enters the home and at the cost of no small self-denial takes upon her the obligations laid down by the one who heard the angel's call and left this sphere of service for that above. This second mother often succeeds if she has the true mother's heart in bringing great happiness to the children under her care. She does her best to make them forget that they are not hers by right of birth. Yet to the end of life there will be moments when a girl's heart will long for the mother in whose arms she was laid, a treasure beyond price, in helpless infancy. The girl without a mother is often forced to make her own decisions. If she makes mistakes they should be pardoned. If she is too willful, too pronounced, even too obstinate who can wonder? She may be a little morbid, this poor child from whose house of love a chill wind of destiny has swept away the roof. If she is the eldest of a group she may have been a mother-sister to those younger than herself, and her father's confidante and aid in his desolate life. Among those who have occupied the place of elder sister to a motherless family none shine with greater luster than the beautiful Catherine Gurney, who at seventeen assumed the responsibility of mothering a large family and of guiding a stately household. One of her younger sisters became widely known in later years as Elizabeth Fry, the great prison philanthropist who antedated others in practical endeavors to improve the condition of women prisoners in England. Two of her brothers, Joseph and Samuel Gurney, were famous for their deeds of noble charity and not one of the entire family circle was narrow or commonplace. They were not slow in praising the sister who gave up so much of her life to the formation of their characters and the brightening of their home.

Elizabeth Barrett was another motherless girl who, before she met the poet who became her husband, Robert Browning, spent years as an invalid in her father's house. That father although affectionate was a domestic tyrant and one cannot but marvel how the girl's splendid genius budded and bloomed under his despotic regime. Very little is said in the memoirs of Mrs. Browning about the mother who was early taken away from her little brood. But I like to think that a large portion of her gentle spirit descended to her gifted daughter.

Yet a mother in heaven may not be so far away from the child she has left. Her influence is no less potent because her voice is hushed. It may be that a daughter remembers more tenderly the precepts of one who is gone than she would were the mother at her side. A deep sacredness invests the mother who is out of sight.

They never quite leave us, our friends who have passed
Through the shadows of death to the sunlight above;
A thousand sweet memories are holding them fast
To the places they blest with their presence and love.

The work which they left and the books which they read
Speak mutely, though still with an eloquence rare;
And the songs that they sung, the dear words that they said,
Yet linger and sigh on the desolate air.

And oft when alone, and as oft in the throng,
Or when evil allures us or sin draweth nigh,
A whisper comes gently, "Nay, do not the wrong,"
And we feel that our weakness is pitied on high.

We toil at our tasks in the burden and heat
Of life's passionate noon; they are folded in peace.
It is well; we rejoice that their heaven is sweet,
And one day for us all the bitter will cease.

We, too, shall go home o'er the river of rest,
As the strong and the lovely before us have gone;
Our sun will go down in the beautiful west.
To rise in the glory that circles the throne.

Until then we are bound by our love and our faith
To the saints who are walking in Paradise fair;
They have passed beyond sight at the touching of death,
But they live, like ourselves, in God's infinite care.

Should it happen to a girl who has had at an early age control of her father's house and much care of her brothers and sisters, to have the reins of authority taken from her grasp and the care placed in the hands of another, let her not repine or act as though she were a martyr. The new mother coming into the place that seemed so sacred to the old will have her difficulties and has her claims. For the sake of her father as well as for the vindication of her own mother's sweetness and strength, the elder daughter at such a time should do everything in her power to smooth the way for the stepmother. On her side the newcomer has it in her power to relieve a burdened girl of great responsibilities, and set her free to live her own life. In an instance where a youthful daughter had bravely carried on everything in the way that her mother would approve, often undertaking tasks beyond her strength, the news that her father was about to marry again came to her as an unlooked-for announcement. She told me that it was like a thunderbolt falling from a clear sky. But at once with rare discretion and gentleness she set about preparing the younger children to meet the new mother with a fitting welcome. She herself led them in this. Later she was enabled to leave home and study for the profession on which her eyes had been set during her mother's lifetime, and she entered on a career of conspicuous usefulness, doing good in a way given to few young women. Years after, she again took up the duties of elder sister to the children of her second mother, when the latter dying left them to her care.

Whatever the circumstances may be the great necessity for all of us is to do the next thing. We are to put aside as unworthy all selfishness. More than anyone else, perhaps the girl who has no mother here should try to live as though at the end of the day she could give the dear mother an account of the day's doings.

Another consolation sometimes comes in the thought of sorrow and trouble, suffering and pain, that a mother has escaped. "I felt as if the world crumbled under my feet," said a daughter alluding to the mother she had lost. "When I looked at my mother's face in the last sleep I felt that my heart was broken, but I have lived long enough to be thankful that her gentle spirit was early taken away from the evil to come. We who were young could better bear the blows of misfortune than she could, after she had reached the meridian."

Still another thought is that the touch of sorrow in our lives enables us to sympathize more deeply with all who suffer than we could have done had we never known grief. We learn sympathy through suffering. No sorrow comes to us except from the hand of a loving Father and it is sent to make nobler, larger, and quicker to respond to the call of humanity.

I heard an old farmer talk one day,
Telling his listeners how,
In the wide, new country far away,
The rainfall follows the plough.

"As fast as they break it up, you see,
And turn the heart to the sun,
As they open the furrows deep and free,
And the tillage is begun,

"The earth grows mellow, and more and more
It holds and sends to the sky
A moisture it never had before,
When its face was hard and dry.

"And so, whenever the ploughshares run,
The clouds run overhead;
And the soil that works and lets in the sun,
With water is always fed."

I wonder if that old farmer knew
The half of his simple word,
Or guessed the message that heavenly true
Within it was hidden and heard?

It fell on my ear by chance that day,
But the gladness lingers now,
To think it is always God's dear way
That the rainfall follows the plough.

Chapter XXIII

Friends and Comrades

IMAGINE yourself cast away on a desert island without a friend. You might have a shelter against the wind, food to eat, and the hope of getting away but the solitude would be insupportable unless you had the good fortune to have three or four of your dearest friends with you. A desert island, Katherine tells us, would suit her very well if Miriam and Phoebe were there too. Life would be shorn of pleasure to most of us and would be as lonely as a desert but for our friends. I feel with Katherine that I could live almost anywhere happily if I had near me a few congenial comrades with whom I might walk and talk and exchange views about books, and plan the day's work, and weave hopes for the morrow.

Should a hundred girls come together at the beginning of a school year, bringing with them nothing but their common youth and brightness, if they were all strangers, some from the North, and some from the South, in a week they would break into groups and the group would divide into twos and threes, and the friends would have found each other out. A girl from California would discover her chosen mate in a girl from Maine, another from Kentucky would prefer as chum somebody from the Back Bay, Boston, and without other explanation than the attractions of affinity, choice spirits would meet and mingle and deepen their joy. This would not in any way detract from the loyalty the school might feel for itself, as a whole, nor would it interfere with the feeling that makes pupils proud of an institution. The congenial girls would inevitably form groups and grow into friendships.

In order to have true friendship there must be corresponding qualities, although contrasts are more likely to make a rounded friendship than are similarities. A grave and sober girl finds her complement in one whose gaiety bubbles up like a fountain. The girl who is reticent and slow of speech often has as her dearest friend a fluent girl who is in danger of talking too much. Beneath superficial contrasts there are resemblances, and bell answers to bell with instant accord.

Whether or not girl friendships invariably last is not a question of much moment. There is such a thing as outgrowing a friend and it is rather a mournful process, unless absence and distance have dulled the sense of possession. When Florence goes to Berlin to study music, and Frances moves to Florida to live in an orange grove and the two are separated for five or six years, they very naturally drift apart. At first letters fly across the ocean with every mail; after a while the girls cease to write regularly, and it may well be that their friendship languishes. Frances is dwelling in a world very different from the world of Florence. Strong natures hold their own through silence and absence, yet it is according to nature that we change with the years and form new ties when we are separated. There are girl-friendships that endure through the years of a lifetime, so that very old women keep on loving one another as they did when they were brown-haired girls sitting side-by-side in the schoolroom.

The important thing about a friendship is not the

question, Shall I love Emily or will Emily love me twenty-five years hence but, Are Emily and I helping one another at this hour? The keynote of true friendship is helpfulness. Am I a good comrade? Do I by every word I say and every deed I do add to the real welfare of my friend? Are we having good times together? I have very little faith in girl-friendships that leave out good times.

A reef to avoid is that of a too exclusive friendship. When Jean cannot live without Mary, and Mary is wretched if a day passes in which she does not see her beloved Jean, something is wrong. Girls would better be on their guard against themselves if they find that they are miserable if a third person comes into their company, and if they are jealous when their dearest friend walks across the campus with her arm around somebody else. In rare instances there exists what may be called the friendship of the parasite. A girl so clings to a friend, so absorbs the friend's thought, and so winds herself about another life that morbidness and disease follow. A parasite may be very beautiful indeed, but it chokes the life of the tree around which it creeps. I am sure there is not a girl in the world who would choose to be a parasite if she realized what a poison-bearing office must be hers. Avoid wild enthusiasms and riotous fancies that make you miserable and forlorn when the beloved object is out of sight.

No little injustice is done unintentionally by those who suppose that young girls are indifferent about friendships with each other, and absorbingly interested only in friendships that have to do with men. Long before the dawn of love there are sweet and devoted friendships that bind girls in a closeness of intimacy entirely apart from the later feeling that belongs to the realm of love and the choosing of comrades for a life partnership. With many girls friendship continues to keep its place in the foreground, and they are never conscious of an unsatisfied want beyond that which friendship supplies. The flame burning on the vestal hearth is pure and clean and there have been women to whom it has furnished light and heat during the years of a brilliant life.

Alice and Phoebe Cary were sisters, and in their relationship found a satisfactory basis for an affection transcending sisterly regard. In passing, it may be noted that girls are not always intimate with their sisters and that sisters may be uncongenial. Incompatibility of temperament and will is hostile to friendship whether it be found in the circle of kindred or in the fellowship of acquaintances. When sisters dearly love and truly appreciate each other, no friendship is so hallowed and beautiful and altogether spontaneous as theirs. A thousand sweet associations dating back to the scarcely remembered days of infancy twine themselves in with a sisterly friendship. One sometimes sees this in a perfection that has not a flaw else it would not be perfect, when the sisters are twins who have drawn breath together from the earliest hour of life.

Years ago in a hospitable home where every Saturday night throngs of agreeable and often highly gifted people gathered, there dwelt two friends, Mary Louise Booth and Annie Wright. These two though outwardly dissimilar had a certain spiritual likeness that was felt by all who knew them. They shared their possessions and their income, lived in unbroken sympathy for years, and made a great many friends happier and better because their friendship did not incline them to be selfish or solitary.

Lucy Stanley and Maria Hare began their friendship when they were little girls, and it endured the vicissitudes of a long life. The story of that sweet friendship perfumes the pages of a book, classic among biographies, *Memorials of a Quiet Life*.

To return to the friendships of girls as they are seen every day shall we glance at what may be called the practical side?

Charlotte and Susan are chums and roommates. Perhaps they have one of those fascinating suites consisting of a sitting room in the center with an alcove or room on either side, so that sleeping arrangements though not very far apart are sufficient to give an assurance of privacy. This is the ideal plan when girls at school or college room together.

In everyone's life there must be the opportunity as there is the need for occasional retirement, and the ability to close a door is as essential to firm friendship as the willingness usually to open the door widely.

When friends live in such proximity they should respect one another's desire for privacy, they should refrain from invading the silent times at night and morning without which the soul cannot thrive, and they should be careful to respect each other's right of property. The early Christians, it is true, had everything in common but this was because the conditions of society and of the infant church made a common fund convenient and brotherly sharing of goods a protection against a common foe. It was not an arrangement intended to be permanent.

When girls cease to regard the individual possessions of their friends and without leave wear each other's clothing, snatch up ribbons, stocks and kerchiefs, seize and carry off a book without asking, friction and annoyance are sure to follow. In home life, too, and everywhere in social intercourse it is a law of good manners not to borrow our friends' belongings without our friends' sanction.

A hint may be given as to the loaning and the prompt repayment of small sums of money by girl friends. I knew a generous girl who was put to serious inconvenience, incurring pecuniary embarrassment through a term at boarding school, because in her first fortnight she lent a good part of her allowance to girls who were tardy in reimbursing her. It is well to keep strict account of financial transactions in friendship, and the friendship is likely to be most enduring into which these obligations do not intrude.

I have heard girls insist with apparent candor that they enjoy being told their faults. They may be sincere, at least they fancy that they are. In the book of Proverbs we are told that the kisses of an enemy are deceitful, while faithful are the wounds of a friend. Unless there is the gravest occasion for doing so, refrain from conversing with your friend about her faults and foibles. The probability is that you have plenty of your own; most of us have. Among the most ungracious offices ever undertaken are the offices of criticism and suggestion between those who stand on the same levels of friendship. Do not think to make your friend love you more deeply by dwelling on her weakness, her awkwardness, her crudeness, or her mistakes. Her mother or her teacher may be called upon to admonish, rebuke, and exhort but as a friend you are expected to be a little blind to that which is unfortunate and to see with great clearness that which is lovely and attractive.

I have doubt as to the depth and worth of a friendship when the parties to it find congenial occupation in criticism. The critical spirit is not one to be cultivated by any of us. "Lucile would be a girl after my own heart," said a woman to me as a beautiful girl left us, "if she were not so critical. In the call she has just finished she has not spoken with unalloyed praise of a single girl among her friends."

If you are aware in yourself of a tendency to criticize or a disposition to see faults, be stern with it and rout it from your character. No surer means of discontent can be planted there. We may safely be frank and uncompromising with our own faults, but it is well to have toleration and patience with the faults of our friends.

"A friend loveth at all times, and a brother is born for adversity." How swift is the impulse to go at once without an instant's delay to our friend who is in sorrow. Friendship is not merely for fair weather. It is not for the days when there is music in the air, when the skies are serene and the flowers are blooming. It is for days of silence and days of storm. Ask yourself if you are of the stuff that will stand by a friend no matter what ill may happen to her, or what disappointment and disaster overtake her on the road. Having loved a friend never cast her out of the sanctuary into which friendship has brought her.

Somebody inquires, How can friendship be helpful if friends are to shrink from plainness of speech? The answer is that a good deal of so-called honesty and plainness of speech is unnecessary if the friends are real. Many things are understood in the realm of friendship without resort to the medium of words. A glance, a handclasp and above all other things an example of Christian living are more potential than language in influencing those one loves. Should a subject arise which is in the nature of an entering wedge as when unfortunately two girls may be competitors for the same prize and one is taken and the other left, or as when two very dear friends love the same man and one is chosen and the other left, the test of friendship is in self-denial and silence. For instance, Estelle and Dorothy whose lives had run side-by-side for years, who seemed to have almost a single soul between them, one summer day met Louis who speedily drifted into a delightful friendship with both girls. Onlookers wondered which of the two he would choose, for it soon became evident that he was to be more than a friend to one. Might it be Dorothy's violet eyes with their glints of heaven, or Estelle's dark ones that were like brown pools in the sunshine that should fix and keep his regard? The spectators sitting here and there in corners of the veranda had their opinions and more than one matron sighed as she reflected that for one of the friends a heartache was inevitable. When finally Louis' engagement to Estelle was announced, Dorothy was first to offer congratulations and by not so much as the flicker of an eyelid did she show that she had suffered disappointment. The friendship remained unimpaired, yet Dorothy's life afterward for many a year was lonely. It is the final test of girl-friendship when it can resign the intangible without allowing an interruption in what has been the stuff of daily life.

Chapter XXIV

Christian Service

FIELDS of Christian service are white to the harvest on every side. The girl who has consecrated her young life to her Friend and Master Jesus Christ looks about her in the flush of her radiant morning and asks earnestly, Where shall I go and what shall I do?

It may be that the answer to her question lies in the direction of foreign missions. In the immense growth of foreign mission work in the last quarter-century, the openings for the labor of single women have wonderfully multiplied. A girl may find her opportunity in teaching either little children in a kindergarten or seniors in a college on the other side of the globe. I think as I write, of a lovely girl who gathers about her a group of brown-faced little maids, with golden chains on neck and wrists, in a high caste school for Hindu girls. Another has found her work in teaching Chinese girls and she tells me that their progress and their rapid mental improvement, their docility and patience, surpass anything she has ever witnessed in teaching at home.

A young woman whose endowment and equipment are of the highest and whose training includes postgraduate work in London and Berlin, after exhaustive study at home, has gone to South Africa and is successfully teaching advanced literature in two languages to pupils there. The demand for teachers of every grade in the foreign mission field is constant, increasing, and imperative.

The young woman may go out if she chooses, and has the preparation requisite for the work, as a medical missionary. The need for the woman doctor in the Far East, on the islands of the sea, everywhere indeed in heathen lands cannot be exaggerated. The customs of Oriental peoples debar male physicians from attendance on women, and for this reason women for centuries have been left to suffer untold agonies or to die prematurely. The medical missionary goes to the women of the East as a ministering angel. It sounds incredible but between hospitals, dispensaries, and outpatients a woman doctor in India or China may attend from three to five thousand patients annually. Sometimes as in the case of the lamented Dr. Eleanor Chestnut the reward of her labors is the martyr's crown. The servant is not above the Master. Our Lord was nailed to the Cross. As they hated Him without cause, so often since the twentieth century began, they have hated and killed His followers. Yet this makes not against, but for missionary work in heathen lands. It accentuates the need.

The woman missionary may be an evangelist, going with a companion or two from village to village, entering lowly homes, preaching Christ to women who come at eventide to the well to draw water, or reading and explaining the Bible to those who have never heard it.

If you wish to be a foreign missionary, dismiss from your mind every illusion of romance. The work is not romantic, far from it. It involves in the first place exile from home and friends for a period of five to seven years. At the end of that period the missionary is in want of her furlough. She will probably spend three-fourths of it on her return in visiting societies and telling the people at home about her work and about the conditions in the distant field to which they send their money. She will find this on sinecure. Her work on the field necessitates hard study of difficult languages with no affinity for her own; it will be interrupted unless she is exceptionally fortunate by illness and fever; she will encounter dirt, degradation, pestilential vapors, torrid heat, or freezing cold; and worse than all, she will feel the deep loneliness of one who is away from the atmosphere of Christianity. Nevertheless, for Christ's sake she will accept every hardship with gladness and she will say as I have heard more than one tired toiler say, with beaming face, Unless you have been a missionary in a foreign land, you have never tasted the deepest joy beneath the sun.

There are never wanting hostile critics to comment unfavorably on the girl who leaves her home to become a foreign missionary. These people wonder that she can forsake her mother or her father or that she cannot find a sphere for her powers in the tenements or in her own neighborhood. If one is convinced that her call to the mission field is genuine and if her parents give their free consent to her choice, she should brush aside as though they were cobwebs the flimsy objections of the unsympathetic.

In presenting herself to a foreign mission board she will be obliged to submit to a severe examination. Mere Christian enthusiasm is not sufficient, although it is important. She will be asked about her education, its thoroughness, what direction it has taken, what languages she has studied and her proficiency in them, about her church membership, and her experience in Christian activity, about her social standing, and her physical health. In sending a worker forth the foreign mission board takes a threefold responsibility: to the church at home, to the workers already in the field, and to the field itself. It must therefore be extremely careful in every particular.

Whatever is said here in regard to foreign mission work applies with equal force to evangelical work at home. If you wish to enter any department of the home mission field you must be fitted intellectually, physically, and spiritually for the work and you will find as many handicaps and as many hardships and, too, as many rewards as in the other.

Both at home and abroad the work of Young Women's Christian Associations is making phenomenally rapid strides. The city work touching the lives of young women in business, the factory extension work reaching out to the toiling operatives in mills and shops, the college work penetrating into institutions of learning far and wide have created what may be called a new profession for Christian women. The work of the resident or the traveling secretary of the Christian Association is akin to that of the missionary and partakes of the same character. It is by no means easy. The traveling secretary covers thousands of miles during the year in keeping her appointments. She makes many addresses, spends hours in laborious personal interviews, must conciliate here, persuade there, and impress everywhere, and she lays her entire womanly force and equipment at the feet of her Lord. The resident secretary is the intimate friend of girls away from home, who bring to her their problems and their trials and who must be counseled, strengthened, and comforted at critical moments. She is the friend, too, of her board of managers and must know how to act in concert with them and how to so bear herself that she shall win the confidence and respect of the community, and thus gain friends who shall sustain her work.

There are at this moment resident secretaries not alone in the cities and villages of America and Europe, but in South America, South Africa, Calcutta, Bombay, Shanghai, Yokohama, and other great foreign centers. The harvest beckons and as yet the laborers are too few.

In schools and colleges, in the Sunday school and the Christian Endeavor Society and Epworth League, here at home, the Christian girl finds pressing need for her ready and willing service. Yet it may be, after all, that the place of her appointment is not anywhere outside of her quiet home life. One may as truly serve God in making a cup of tea for a tired mother, in caring for a fretful infant that its mother may go to church, in hearing the lessons of a little boy who is puzzled over his homework, in reading to a friend whose eyes are dim, in entertaining a shut-in who spends day after day behind the bars of infirmity, in singing for the convalescents in a hospital ward, or in teaching a Bible class in a prison, as in a more conspicuous field of effort. To each of us the call comes to serve the Lord in doing the next thing. We may best illustrate the Christian principle within us, sometimes by bearing a keen disappointment with patience, sometimes by abandoning a cherished plan, sometimes by scrubbing a kitchen floor, or by making a loaf of perfect bread.

We are living in times so full of swift change and of absorbing interest and of widening opportunity that we cannot escape service of some sort. It is a thought worth taking to heart, girls, that if you are not serving Christ you are helping His enemies. If you are not bringing in His kingdom of love you are aiding the advancement of the kingdom of evil in the world.

The words of Julia Ward Howe's battle hymn ring in our ears like a challenge:

He is sounding forth the trumpet that shall never call retreat,
He is sifting out the hearts of men before His Judgment Seat,
Oh, be swift my soul to answer Him, be jubilant my feet,
For God is marching on.

Are you a daughter of the King? I do not mean are you a member of the beautiful order of which the badge is a purple ribbon and a tiny silver cross. If you are that it is all the better, but are you to your own consciousness and in sweet assurance a daughter of the King of Heaven? The King's daughter is all glorious within. If you belong to Jesus Christ, your heart is filled with such gladness as no one knows until she has placed her hand in the hand that was pierced.

You do not make the mistake of imagining that your service is all where it can be seen of men. You have your silent hours at morning or evening where you sit as Mary did and listen for the word the Master has to say to you. With Mary you have chosen the better part; with Martha, although you may be cumbered with earthly care, you yield entire trust to what the Lord has to say and you are ready to do His bidding. It was to Martha at Bethany that Jesus said, "I am the resurrection and the life. He that believeth in Me, though he were dead, yet shall he live."

A part of Christian service never to be omitted is ours when we are alone with God, in the morning watch, in the twilight hour, sometimes in the noontide we bring our empty cups to the Lord that He may fill them. Unless those cups are constantly replenished in communion with heaven, they will never be full enough to overflow for the refreshment of the world.

You remember that Brother Lawrence practiced in his daily life and in his most humble services the thought of the presence of Christ. If we carry this thought with us, every day will be beautiful and happy in the light of His countenance.

I have known girls who attached too much importance to what may be styled the paraphernalia of Christian service. They insisted on having not only a little sanctuary in reality in their rooms but in fitting up corners and alcoves for devotional purposes, and so attached did they grow to these that they could never be happy away from them. Others think too much about times and seasons. Externals may be useful in their way, but the soul that is always in touch with the divine Friend may find a sanctuary anywhere. The seat on the deck of a steamer with crowds nearby, or in the rushing train, may be for the moment a retreat whence one calls upon God. Swifter than light or electricity may be the soul's appeal to the Lord and the Lord's answer. Cultivate the habit of trust, believe that nothing is too little for the Lord to notice; tell Him the longings and the heartaches and commit to Him without a fear the whole of your life for this world and the next.

Your Christian service will not end with this short life. It is to go on and on forever in that bright world of which it is said that there His servants shall serve Him.

With Adelaide Anne Proctor shall we not say,

I do not ask, O Lord, that life may be
A pleasant road;
I do not ask that Thou wouldst take from me
Aught of its load.

I do not ask that flowers should always spring
Beneath my feet:
I know too well the poison and the sting
Of things too sweet

For one thing only, Lord, dear Lord, I plead,
Lead me aright—
Though strength should falter, and though heart should bleed—
Through peace to light.

I do not ask, O Lord, that Thou shouldst shed
Full radiance here:
Give but a ray of peace, that I may tread
Without a fear.

I do not ask my cross to understand,
My way to see;
Better in darkness just to feel Thy hand,
And follow Thee.

Joy is like a restless day, but peace divine
Like quiet night:
Lead me, O Lord, till perfect day shall shine,
Through peace to light.